RAG RUGS

RAG
RUGS

Techniques in
Contemporary Craft Projects

Juju Vail

CHARTWELL
BOOKS, INC.

To David and Ollie Wren

A QUINTET BOOK

Published by Chartwell Books
A Division of Book Sales, Inc.
114, Northfield Avenue
Edison, New Jersey 08837

This edition produced for sale in the U.S.A.,
its territories and dependencies only.

ISBN 0-7858-0658-X

This book was designed and produced by
Quintet Publishing Limited
6 Blundell Street
London N7 9BH

Creative Director: Richard Dewing
Designer: Isobel Gillan
Project Editor: Diana Steedman
Editor: Samantha Gray
Photographer: Keith Waterton
Illustrator: Elsa Godfrey

Typeset in Great Britain by
Central Southern Typesetters, Eastbourne
Manufactured in Singapore
by Eray Scan Pte Ltd
Printed in Singapore
by Star Standard Industries (Pte) Ltd

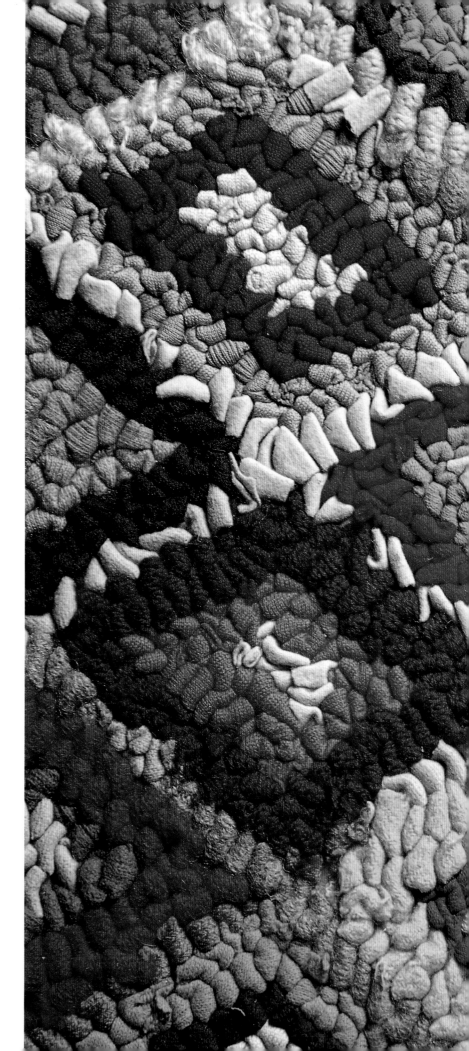

OPENING PAGE

MYTHOLOGICAL BEAST hooked picture
by Lynne Stein (measures 13 x 12in).

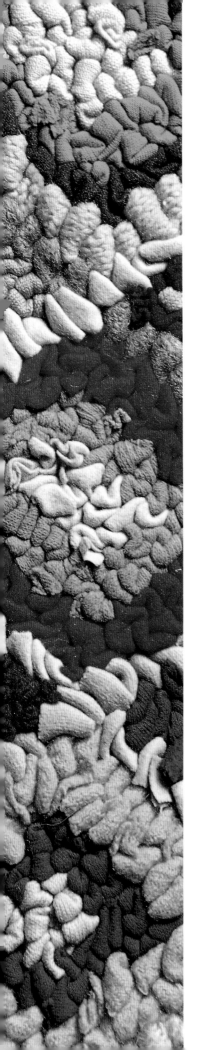

CONTENTS

Foreword 6

THE EVOLUTION OF RAG RUGS 7

PREPARATIONS AND FINISHINGS 19

HOOKED RAG RUGS 29
 The Flying Gardener Children's Rug 36
 Hen in the Garden Rug 39
 Dress Pin 42
 Heart Rug 44
 Golden Hamstrings Runner 47
 "There Was Nothing On It But Tea" 50
 Hooked Hat 54
 Cottage Garden Rug 58
 Whale Rug 61
 Small Scalloped Rug 64
 Coat On A Line Picture 68
 Angel Bench Cushion 71
 Neo-classical Rug 74
 Diamond Rug 77

PRODDED RAG RUGS 81
 Moonlit Forest Rug 86
 Fire Rug 89

BRAIDED RAG RUGS 93
 Braided Rug 96
 Hearth Rug 99

APPLIQUÉ RAG RUGS 102
 Pieced Felt Rug 108
 Mosaic Felt Rug 111

TEMPLATES 114

Appendix 124

Acknowledgments 127

Index 128

FOREWORD

I discovered rag rugs while studying design in England. I was looking for a versatile textile technique that wasn't expensive and which would allow me to express my ideas. I remembered hooked rugs from my native Canada, and thought of their quirkiness and vibrant colors and the enormous variety of designs. Could a traditional craft technique be so idiosyncratic, or was I just homesick?

▲ *Hooked rug (measures 39 x 23in, mid-twentieth century).*

◀ *Detail of* JENNY'S RUG. *Chris Oakenfull's hooking, outlining the motifs in her design.*

On my next trip to Canada, I visited museums and looked at old hooked rugs. Each rug, whether it had been made from a pattern or was a unique design, showed the ingenuity and originality of its maker. Here was an endless source of inspiration!

I studied the rugs to learn how they were made; I took photographs and made notes. When I returned to my studio in England I began experimenting. It didn't take long to realize that I had discovered the versatile technique that I sought. And the materials could not have come more cheaply! I went to jumble sales with my husband; we filled garbage bags with clothes made from bright, sparkly, and exciting fabrics. At the checkout till, no one bothered to add up the cost of every garment – they just charged $5.00 for as much as we could carry. I had enough material to last for years within a month of beginning the craft! Of course, I did have to move to a larger studio.

In this book there are shown many photographs of the old rugs that originally inspired me as well as rugs by new makers that are influenced by contemporary aesthetics, issues and 'green' thinking. The rug makers who contributed to this book, both historical and contemporary, come from many different backgrounds. Some are art school trained, others are self-taught or were taught by members of their family or community.

The projects are designed to inspire you. You may make them exactly as they are designed, adapt them to suit your own interior, or just read the instructions to discover how different rug makers approach their craft.

Four rag rug techniques are featured in this book: hooking, prodding, braiding, and appliqué. These require little or no experience of textile crafts. There are other kinds of rag rugs, such as knitted, crocheted, and woven rugs, that are not described because they require experience with textile construction techniques. However, if you are skilled in one of these areas, the chapters on the design, preparation, and finishing of rag rugs will provide you with some ideas for making other types of rag rugs.

This book is divided into two parts. The first part outlines the four rag rug techniques described above. Information follows on the design, preparation, and finishing methods common to all the rag rug techniques.

The second part of this book is divided into four sections. The first section describes the technique for hooked rugs and the projects include rugs, cushions, hats, jewelry, and wall hangings. In the second section the technique for making prodded rugs is described and there are two prodded rug projects to make. The third section shows how to make braided rugs and the projects include both a braided rug and a hooked rug with a braided border. In the final section you can discover how to make felt appliquéd rugs. There are two appliquéd rug projects which include instructions for making felt.

To make the projects featured in this book you need have no previous experience of textile crafts and a mastery of the simple techniques described can provide the basis for a lifetime of experimentation and creative satisfaction.

▲ Laura Secord
hooked vest by Barbara Klunder.

▼ Fact and Fiction
hooked cushions by Janice McLaren.

THE EVOLUTION OF RAG RUGS

Rugs made from remnants of fabric, yarn, and fleece are common to many cultures. They are a craft born of necessity. However, this has never limited the originality or creativity of their designs.

In nineteenth-century North America, carpets imported from Europe were too costly for most people. Rag rugs proved to be an economical solution to covering drafty floors. Readily available burlap sacks provided rug backings, while the remnants of cloth, too worn for quilt making, were suitable for a rug pile. Rag rugs were relatively quick to work and were made in the evenings or seasons when weather made farming or fishing impossible. The variety of possible techniques, color, and designs ensured that these rugs were a source of pride to their makers as well as being useful.

North American communities making rag rugs were often rural and sometimes very isolated. Similar techniques with different names and different tools developed in each community. The terms used in this book are the most popular.

Like other textile crafts, rag rugs have declined in popularity as commercial products replace them and communities change. However, new interest in this absorbing craft is growing alongside recycling and 'green' movements and among those using traditional crafts to express their creativity.

▼ BOXED RED DRESS
by Susan Lindsay (measures 26 x 16¼in).

◀ *Selection of rag rugs.*

HOOKED RUGS

Hooked rugs are made by drawing loops of rag strips or yarn through a burlap ground fabric. The surface can be as refined as a tapestry, or it can be crude and primitive, or colorful and tactile. Hooking is the most versatile of the rag rug techniques and arguably one of the most versatile textile techniques. A hooked rug does not have to be worked sequentially, one row at a time, the way a tapestry does; the rug maker can work freely, and unpick areas if necessary. Anything that can be drawn on the surface of burlap can be 'painted' with hooked rags.

Traditional hooked rugs (or mats as they were commonly called) were usually no larger than the burlap feed sack used to make them, about 2 x 3 feet and were rarely square. Sometimes long, narrow runners for the hallway or stair were constructed from a series of sacks. These typically measured 8 feet x 19 inches.

Along the Eastern coast of North America and in French Canada, hooked mats adorned the floors of every room in a house. There would be as many as ten or more to a room, each of a different pattern and color. The best mats were saved for the parlor or bedrooms. These were usually worked in a brightly colored design and the hooking would be especially fine. The kitchen floor was covered in mats with simple geometric designs, or worn mats from other rooms in the house, since in the kitchen they were washed frequently. Rug patterns were drawn on burlap sacks with a piece of chalk, a piece of burnt coal or a stick taken from the stove.

When and where rug hooking began is not accurately documented. Some textile historians claim that there is a British-Scandinavian origin, while others believe that the craft is indigenous to North America. The most convincing proof lies in favor of a North American invention. The non-existence of early examples of hooked rugs or of literature and records about hooking in museums and private collections in Great Britain supports this. Early rugs are traced to the Maritime provinces of Canada, Quebéc, and New England, where the craft probably developed simultaneously. However, examples of hooked rugs made in Britain and throughout North America are common from the late nineteenth century.

▲ *Maria Warning from Perth County, Ontario, made a number of rugs in the late 1800s. (Rugs measure 54 x 25½in and 24 x 42in).*

▲ *This hooked rug was probably made from a stamped burlap pattern. Accurate dates of old rag rugs are difficult to establish since they may refer to the year in which they were hooked or commemorate an important event (measures 57½ x 29in).*

▲ COCK-A-DOODLE-DOO
hooked rug by Anita Langham
(measures 27½ x 24in).

◄ EAGLE *circular hooked rug trimmed with*
fleece by Jenni Stuart-Anderson
(measures 35in in diameter).

▼ LAURA SECORD *hooked rug by*
Barbara Klunder (measures 48 x 84in).

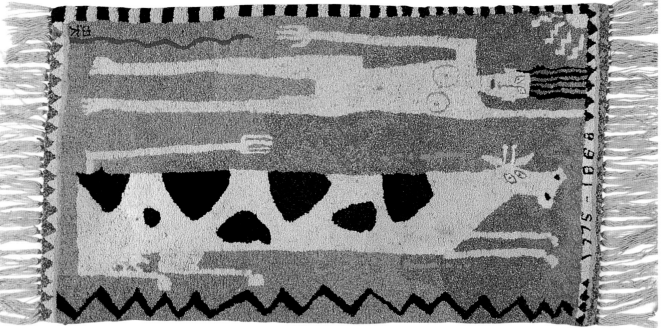

► *Mennoite made hooked rug*
(measures 20 x 32in, early twentieth century).

▲ MERMAID *hooked picture*
by Lynne Stein (measures 18 x 12in).

► *Hooked map of Newfoundland*
by the Grenfell Industries, Labrador
(measures 42 x 31in).

THE EVOLUTION OF RAG RUGS

▶ *Hooked rug, adapted from a painting by a popular Quebec artist George-Edouard Tremblay. Tremblay ran a workshop converting his designs into hooked rugs which were sold in Canada and the United States (measures 30 x 33in, c 1930s).*

▼ *This rug was hooked by nuns in Québec. The change of hooking direction and color in the sky and water make this mat quirky and unusual (measures 35 x 55in).*

Prior to the arrival of burlap in North America, hooked rugs were made from a coarse linen which had some of its warp and weft threads removed to make a firm, open-weave fabric. Examples of rugs made on a linen backing fabric are uncommon. Most surviving rugs were made with a commercially woven burlap foundation which means they cannot have been made much before 1850. The jute fiber of which

burlap is woven was introduced to America and Europe from India in about 1820. Between 1854 and 1857 English-made, steam-driven machines were installed in Calcutta factories, and soon afterwards burlap sacking became commonplace in North America. The easy availability of burlap marks the beginnings of rug hooking as a popular craft.

Hooked rugs grew in popularity throughout the 1800s. In the 1870s stamped burlap rug patterns became readily available, further popularizing the craft until commercial carpets replaced them in the 1920s.

▲ *Hooked rug from Québec (measures 38 x 27in).*

◄ *This rug is one of a pair of hooked runners. Pairs of runners were made to cover the hallway and stairs (measures 100 x 22in).*

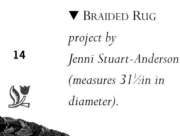

▼ BRAIDED RUG
*project by
Jenni Stuart-Anderson
(measures 31½in in
diameter).*

PRODDED RUGS

Prodded rugs are made from long strips of fabric poked through a burlap ground. The effect is similar to hooked rugs but the technique produces a rug with a longer, shaggier pile. Prodded rugs are more common in Great Britain than in North America and are known by various names to different communities – 'prodded', 'poked', and 'proggie' are the most common terms.

Prodded rug designs are usually worked in simpler designs than hooked rugs. They often included black borders made from old stockings or men's suits and a center filled with random colored strips known as 'hit or miss' patterning. Another common prodded design was a large diamond in the center of a rug.

BRAIDED RUGS

Braided rugs are made from braided fabric strips stitched together. The rugs are usually round or oval in shape but the braids can be stitched to make square, rectangular, and other shapes as well. Their beauty lies in the choice of material and the subtle color changes that are achieved when one strand of a braid is changed at a time.

Along with fabric braided rugs, old rope and jute were also transformed into braided rugs. Rope was unraveled and then the strands braided and coiled into a rug.

Braided borders are common on many old hooked, knitted, and crocheted rugs. This feature was typical of the rugs made by the Shaker community in America.

APPLIQUED RUGS

Rugs for the floor were not common in early eighteenth-century colonial homes. However, an object known as a 'rug' but used to decorate the bed was common in most homes. These appliquéed bed rugs eventually took their place on the floor, originally by the fireplace to protect the floor from cinders, but later becoming area rugs. Area rugs were worked in an almost endless variety of needlework techniques before the invention of rug hooking which then became the most popular method for creating a floor rug.

The best-known nineteenth-century appliquéd and embroidered carpet is a 12 x 13½-foot carpet made in Castleton, Vermont, by Zeruah Higley Guernsey Caswell between 1833 and 1835. The rug has 76 squares plus a removable hearth rug section, each embroidered in chain stitch with a different motif. Most of the colorful designs, all on a black ground, are of flowers or leaves, but the maker has also included shells, birds, butterflies, a young couple, and several squares with puppies and cats.

The appliquéd rugs in this book are made by stitching woolen fabric, or similar hardwearing, thick fabric shapes, to a woolen ground fabric supported by a burlap lining. Felt provides the perfect fabric for appliqué as its edges do not fray when cut and therefore do not need to be turned under when stitched in place. The chapter on appliqué rugs includes instructions on how to make felt from woolen fabrics. It also includes instructions for some simple decorative embroidery stitches.

RAG RUG DESIGN

There is no limit to the variety of rag rug designs. The rugs in this book show the flexibility of the craft with designs that are decorative, narrative, painterly, sculptural, or conceptual.

Traditional rug designs included a wide variety of themes. Geometric designs were among the most common because rug makers could follow the grid inherent in the weave of the burlap and therefore did not need to draw out their rugs. Designs featuring farm animals and pets were also common. One rug maker is said to have held her cat to the burlap while her husband drew round it. Flower and

◀ FISHES AND ROSES
*hooked picture
by Lynne Stein
(measures 45 x 30in).*

▼ *Hooked rug made to
commemorate a 25th
anniversary, by
Barbara Klunder
(measures 5 x 4in).*

plant themes were popular, and large leaves could be traced on to burlap to provide simple designs. Slogans and figures also appeared in old rag rugs.

The following suggestions and guidelines offer one approach to designing for rag rugs.

I begin the design process by deciding how the rug will be used. Will it hang on a wall or be in use on a floor? If it is a floor

▲ *Hooked and felt appliqué samplers.*

rug, where will it be? These decisions influence the technique, scale, and imagery of the design. Floor rugs are either viewed at an angle or from directly above at a distance the height of the viewer. Since the viewer is usually at least 5 feet away from the rug, a large, bold design is easier to understand than a small, detailed one. Wall

◄ REACH TO THE STARS
hooked rug by Lu Mason (measures 72 x 36in).

hangings can be designed to be viewed from one direction. However, a floor rug will probably be viewed from every direction, as the viewer moves around the room. Its design should therefore be considered from each direction.

My designs are hybrids of my 'samplers', sketches, and scrapbooks. These methods of collecting design information complement each other. The 'samplers' provide new ideas, techniques, and surprises, while the sketches and scrapbooks reflect my conscious interests.

When I have rug sketches and 'samplers' that I am satisfied with I make a small painting of the design. I do not expect the rug to be an accurate representation of the painting. I let the materials influence the direction of my work, using my painting, placed under an acetate sheet marked with a grid, as a guideline.

If drawing intimidates you, try making a rug design using fabric collage. Pieces of fabric can be 'glued' to a backing using the double-sided fusing method described in the appliqué projects. By using printed, textured, and plain fabric, you may find your collage suggests a variety of materials and techniques.

Sometimes it is necessary to enlarge a rug design to its full-size before making it into a rug. This offers an opportunity to see the scale of a design in relation to other aspects of the interior. If adjustments to the composition, size, or scale need to be made, tracing paper can be used to recopy the design.

▲ *Hooked sampler by Juju Vail.*

▼ *Fabric collages*

PREPARATIONS AND FINISHINGS

TOOLS

Rag rugs require very few tools. I use only a simple hook, frame, and a pair of scissors to make my hooked rugs. Many rug tools can be made from household items.

The tools and materials required for hooked, prodded, braided, and appliquéd rugs vary slightly. Each project lists its requirements along with a few optional accessories to make it easier to complete.

Hooks

Some kind of hooking tool is necessary to make a hooked rug. In the nineteenth-century rural communities where rug hooking was popular, hooks were hand made from a piece of wood which held a nail, chiseled to form a hook. The hook used for making rag rugs has a short shank and does not have a latch. Very few craft shops supply rag rug hooks but they can be bought through mail order distributors (see page 125 for Suppliers).

◀ BEAUTIFUL RED DRESS
*hooked rug by Janice McLaren
(measures 48 x 29in).*

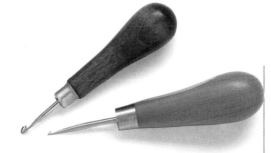

◀ *Primitive rug hook,
extra-fine rug hook.*

Most of the hooking in this book is done with a 'primitive' size hook. This is the tool I recommend buying. An extra fine hook is used for hooking with yarns or narrow fabric strips such as in the Dress Pin project (page 42). The shuttle hook and the punch needle perform 'hooking' functions. They can make work faster to complete but they are used on the wrong side of the rug, which makes work difficult to evaluate as you go along. They also limit the width of the rag strip.

▼ *Shuttle hook*

Prodding Tool

Prodding tools are used for making prodded rugs. Anything that can poke rag strips through the burlap ground fabric can be used: a knitting needle or a bradawl are adequate. Wooden and steel prodding tools can be bought through mail order distributors and are more comfortable to work with.

▼ *Prodding tool*

▲ *Rotary cutter*

▶ *Fabric stripper*

Cutters

One of the most time-consuming activities in making a rag rug is cutting the rag fabric into strips or pieces suitable for hooking, prodding, braiding or appliqué. I have tried using a cloth stripper and a rotary cutter but, for hooking, I still prefer to cut strips individually, with scissors, as I go along as this gives the greatest flexibility. If I am using a woven fabric that can be torn along the grain line, I will tear it instead.

I fold the fabric and cut several strips at one time to make the job faster.

There are a number of cloth strippers on the market. They are great for cutting fabrics to an even width. However, they can be frustrating if you like to use a variety of fabrics (they don't cut light fabrics easily and synthetics blunt their blades quickly) or different widths (changing the blade width is slow).

A rotary cutter and mat can be useful for quickly making strips of any width. However, they require ample cutting space and cannot, therefore, be used while sitting at a hooking frame.

Frames

A frame holds the burlap taut, making it easier to hook or prod rags. An adjustable frame wraps the excess burlap and/or completed rug around its beams so that you can get one hand underneath your rug and one hand above it at all times.

There are several points to consider when choosing a rug frame:

≈ The tighter the tension of the burlap the easier it is to work quickly. Look for a frame that makes it easy to achieve a very taut tension.

≈ Since you cannot see the entire rug as you work on it, you will need to take the burlap off the frame frequently for evaluation as you work. Look for a frame that allows you to do this easily and does not require staples.

≈ Since the burlap is rolled under the frame as it is worked, the length of the frame expands, but the width should be at least 39–47 inches, to give a reasonable number of size options for your rug. Handmade frames can usually be made to fit your width requirements.

You can purchase custom-made frames or those specifically for rug hooking from mail order distributors (see page 125 for Suppliers). This can be costly so you may want to try hooking on a wooden canvas stretcher first. Canvas stretchers are available from art supply stores and come in a variety of sizes. A simple frame can be made from a stretcher by stapling the burlap to the frame, and then pulling all four sides taut. Bear in mind that this method will not produce as quick results as using a specialist rug frame and will not be as comfortable to use. It is not necessary to buy a canvas stretcher as large as the finished rug as the rug can be hooked a little at a time, staples pulled out, then the burlap repositioned before you continue hooking. Even with a frame the rug will need repositioning as it is worked.

◀ MURPHY *hooked rug by Louisa Creed (measures 53 x 39in).*

▼ ART NUNS *hooked rug by Nancy Edell (measures 34 x 49½in).*

▲ *G-clamps*

▼ JONI *hooked rug by Lizzie Reakes. Inspired by Joni Mitchell's* Blue *album, Lizzie used colors of blue to create the multi-dimensional pattern (measures 39in diameter).*

For most rug making an embroidery hoop is inadequate, but it may be acceptable for hooking small pieces with an extra fine hook.

Miscellaneous

You need a supply of threads and needles. A 5-inch long mattress needle and heavy linen carpet thread are helpful. In addition, a long metal or wooden yard stick is useful for drawing the rug dimensions and pattern grids on to the burlap. A rug frame can be supported on the backs of chairs but trestles and G-clamps make hooking and prodding arrangements more comfortable.

A latex adhesive is often used to coat the back of rugs. It has several purposes: it makes the rag strips impossible to pull out, the burlap more hardwearing, and it gives the rug a slip-proof backing which is important if you use your rugs on wooden or tile floors. It can be purchased through mail order or at a hardware store as a latex carpet adhesive, used for gluing carpet tiles in place.

Thick and thin markers in at least three colors are useful for drawing rug patterns on to burlap. Finally, an iron and sewing machine are helpful additions to a rug maker's workshop.

MATERIALS

Rag rugs have the simplest fabric requirements. Old hooked, prodded, and sewn rugs were made on burlap feed sacks. The rug pile was constructed from used clothes and household fabrics, scraps left over from sewing, the jute from burlap sacks, and rough unspun wools. Today we have stronger ground fabrics and an abundance of 'rag' materials for making rugs.

Ground Fabrics

Hooked, prodded, and appliquéd rugs all require a ground fabric for making the rug on. With hooked and prodded rugs the ground fabric holds the rug pile, while stitched rugs use it to mount the appliquéd design. The traditional ground fabric for all these rugs was jute burlap and it is still popular today. It comes in a variety of weights, widths, and colors. The most useful width will depend on the dimensions of your finished rug. The weights include a common 10-ounce weight and a finer weight. The finer weight is stronger but may make hooking or prodding with thick rag strips more difficult.

Stronger ground fabrics are sometimes required by rugs made from narrower strips. A monks cloth or natural linen can be used.

Lining Fabrics

Rugs may be lined with burlap, or printed, dyed, or plain cotton fabrics. A recycled fabric may also be suitable. This is a matter of personal choice.

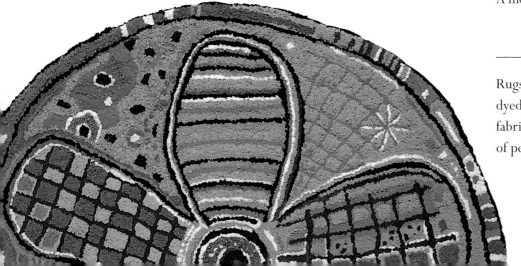

Rug Materials

The choice of materials for hooked, prodded, braided, and appliquéd rugs is almost endless: old clothing, used blankets, towels, sweaters, rugs, yarns, elastic bands, twisted paper, plastic bags, tape, straw, wrapping foils, dental floss, candy wrappers, fur, or feathers are all possibilities. Of course, new materials can also be used but will be more costly.

Recycled fabrics are an economical source for rug making and can offer surprising design choices. Many rug makers prefer to collect fabrics in one fiber family, for instance only pure wools. It is often said that synthetic fibers, like polyester and acrylic, will wear more quickly than natural fibers. However, a variety of fabrics work well together and, when the pile is densely hooked or prodded, synthetics and natural fibers wear equally well. Many synthetics are actually stronger than natural fibers. I recommend setting aside any preferences for natural fibers in hooked and prodded rugs – if a material gives the look you want then it is fine to use. The exception to this rule is with felted rugs. Felt can only be made from pure wool fabrics.

Mail order distributors (see page 125 for Suppliers) sell wool flannels made especially for hooking. These are sold in a large range of colors or you can buy a white flannel and dye it to match your hooking requirements. These give even and predictable results.

Dyes can be used to alter the color of any of your rags. Experiment with dyeing printed and plain fabrics in different dye baths. This can make a subtle range of earth-toned or bright colors. Follow manufacturer's directions or consult a book on dyeing for controlled results.

▲ *Hooked samples and the fabrics that made them.*

▼ *A variety of materials for making rag rugs.*

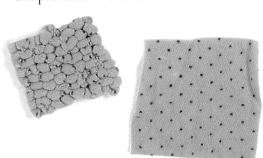

Preparing the 'Rags'

To prepare used clothing and household textiles for rug making, wash them thoroughly with detergent and fabric softener and allow to dry. For clothes, cut the sleeves off bodies and cut the bodies open at side and shoulder seams. Cut off

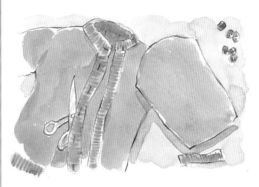

the seams, remove any ribbings, buttons, pockets, edgings, zippers, and trims. You will then have flat pieces of 'rag' fabric ready for making into rugs.

Sort your rags into different color families and store them in clear plastic bags so that you can find appropriate fabrics easily.

▼ *Design for rug with an acetate grid overlay.*

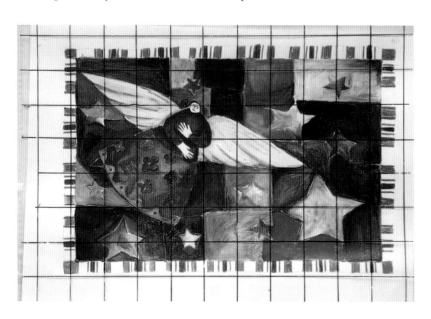

ENLARGING AND TRANSFERRING DESIGNS

There were many ingenious methods of transferring designs to burlap before stamped designs became available. Rug makers copied designs from neighbors' rugs or printed textiles by using a needle to punch through the design to a piece of paper underneath. They would then cut the paper design out and use it as a template to trace on to their own rug. In the 1870s stamped burlap rug patterns came into popular use. However, many rugs were still made from traditional patterns or those of self-invention.

To make most of the rugs in this book you will need to scale up the design and transfer it to burlap:

1 Begin by making a grid acetate overlay: draw a grid of 1 inch squares on to clear acetate using a permanent marker. Designs from this book, greeting cards, old photographs or any design can be photocopied with the acetate overlay to provide a guideline for scaling up designs.

2 Work out the finished dimensions of the rug based on a multiple of the design. For instance a design that measures 10 x 8 inches and has a scale ratio of 1:3 will make a finished rug of 30 x 24 inches, three times the size of the design. If you want your rug to be a different size than the measurements given for the pattern, simply change the scale ratio. For example if you want this rug to measure 38 x 30½ inches, the scale ratio becomes 1:3.8.

3 Draw the finished dimensions on to the burlap in red marker pen. Scale up the grid by the same ratio used to achieve the rug measurements and draw this with the red marker as well.

4 Using the grid as a guide, draw the design on to the burlap in a green marker. This does not take artistic ability, just a little care. If you make a mistake draw the correct line in a darker color marker like black.

Alternatively, you can scale up the design on to paper and then transfer it to the burlap using one of the transfer pencils or markers available, following the manufacturer's directions. You could also make templates for the main motifs in a design and trace these on to the burlap as we have in the *Heart* rug project (page 44).

MOUNTING THE BACKING FABRIC ON A RUG FRAME

If you are using a frame made especially for rug making follow the manufacturer's instructions for mounting the burlap on to the frame. To mount burlap on to a canvas stretcher frame:

1 Lay the burlap flat on the floor and position the frame on top, allowing enough room at the edges to fold the fabric over the frame. Be sure to line up the straight of the fabric grain with one side of the frame.

2 Staple the fabric at one corner of the frame. Then, working along the first side of the frame and keeping the grain

line parallel, staple the fabric at the center and second corner of the frame. Then add staples between these three at 2-inch intervals.

3 Pulling the fabric as taut as possible, stretch the burlap over the opposite edge of the frame, fold it back over the edge and staple it at the center of this side. Then, moving 2 inches to the right of the center staple, again pull the fabric as taut as possible, keeping the grain and frame aligned, and staple. Move to the left of the center staple and repeat this process, stapling about 2 inches apart, and finishing with a staple in each corner.

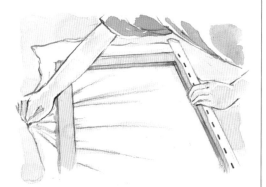

4 Continue in the same way around the third and fourth sides of the frame, pulling the fabric taut and making sure the grain lines stay straight.

▲ Hooked rug made by Maria Warning (measures 54 x 25 ½in).

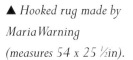

WORKING POSITION

It is important to avoid back and wrist strain while making a rug. Stop work at least once every 20 minutes and stretch out your arms. If you are getting a cramp, stop working. A good working position should prevent discomfort.

Before starting, set aside a suitable space to work. Prepare two supports for your rug frame, ideally a pair of adjustable height trestles. Use four G-clamps to secure the frame to the supports while working. When you are seated at the frame, the rug should be high enough to work with one arm resting naturally above the rug and one below. You should be able to reach the rag strips underneath the burlap without straining for them.

When the hooking becomes too distant to read comfortably, work from the other side of the frame, or move your rug along the frame.

LINING A RUG

Many of the rugs in this book are lined with burlap which is glued to the back of the rug with a latex adhesive. This makes a strong, easy and slip-proof backing. However, once your rug back is coated with latex adhesive, you cannot make changes to the design. It also makes a wall hanging heavier and traditionalists argue that old rugs were never coated with latex. Some of the projects here recommend a cotton lining fabric.

USEFUL STITCHES

The following stitches are useful for attaching linings to rugs and completing the projects:

Rug Back Stitch

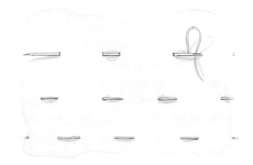

This stitch is used for securing a lining fabric to the entire back surface of a rug. Use a long mattress needle and work on the right side of the lining fabric. Secure the thread with a few stitches in the same spot. Take a short stitch backward, about ¼ inch and insert the needle through the lining fabric and the rug, without going through to the other side of the rug. Bring the needle out 1 inch along. Repeat back and forth until you have completed a row across the rug. Work parallel lines about 1½ inches apart.

Ladder Stitch

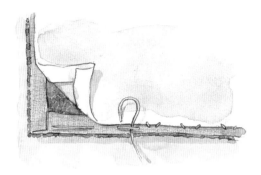

This is a useful stitch for when you want to sew a hemmed lining to a rug back. Work on the right side of the lining fabric. Turn under the hem allowance of the lining along one edge and press. Place this over the hem allowance of the rug on the back side of the rug, and pin at right angles to the seam. Insert the needle inside the fold of the lining hem and take a small stitch across the join through the under layer.

Slip Stitch

Slip stitch holds two folded edges of fabric together and is useful, for example, when joining piping. Work on the right side of the fabric. Fold and press the turning to the wrong side of the fabric. Place the two folded edges parallel to each other. Slip the needle inside the fold on one edge and secure the thread with a couple of back stitches on top of each other. Take a small stitch inside the folded edge, sliding the needle along inside the fold for ¼ inch.

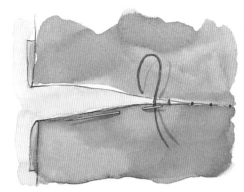

Bring the needle out of the fold and insert it into the other piece of fabric exactly opposite the point where the needle emerged. Catch a couple of threads from the opposite piece of fabric to join the two pieces together.

Herringbone Stitch

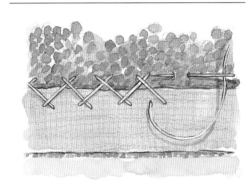

Herringbone stitch is a flat stitch. It is useful for stitching the hem of a rug to its ground fabric. Press the rug hem to the wrong side and work from left to right. With the needle pointing right to left take a horizontal stitch through the flat layer of fabric, picking up just a couple of threads. Move the needle to the right and take a diagonal stitch again, right to left, making cross stitches across the hem edge.

▶ *Detail of* FLYING GARDENER RUG. *A chocolate bar wrapper has been used to hook the gold foil paw of a cat.*

HOOKED RAG RUGS

There are as many different styles of hooked rag rugs as there are styles of handwriting. Some rug hookers aim for neat, evenly spaced loops while others let the rag fabrics dictate the shape and style of the rug. Variations in style depend on the size and type of fabric scraps used, the length of the loop, the height of the pile, whether the pile is cut or uncut, the direction of the hooking, and other quirks of the rug maker's style.

▲ *Maria Warning from Perth County, Ontario, made a number of rugs in the late 1800s, that bore her distinctive style. The motifs in her rugs sat on backgrounds of "hit and miss" colors and included borders of diagonal "hit and miss" patterning.*

◄ *Many unusual materials can be used in hooked rugs. This detail of a rug includes a feather boa and plastic bags.*

Old rugs can sometimes be traced to a particular maker or area by studying the style in which they were executed. For instance, the rugs made by German settlers in Waldoboro, Maine, during the nineteenth century, were hooked from the threads of burlap sacks, and the loops were hooked and clipped to varying heights to produce a sculptured pile. Rugs from Chéticamp, Nova Scotia, were hooked from fine one-ply yarns, while the Grenfell mission, in Labrador, made rugs from dyed silk and nylon stockings, which gave them a detailed pile and distinctive colors.

Since the 1960s hooked rugs have become more uniform and less individual in their style. This may be attributed to commercial pressures to promote new fabrics and yarns above recycled ones; after all, the only necessary equipment for making a hooked rug is a simple hook, burlap, scissors, and an assortment of old clothes.

With the recent enthusiasm for recycling, hooked rag rugs have attracted new interest. Many contemporary rug hookers are unaware of the conventions arising from the commercialization of the craft and have found their own styles. Explore the techniques described in this book and, with practice, you will develop a style of your own.

The Choice of Fabrics

The choice of material can dictate the hooking style and make a dramatic difference to the finished rug. Anything that can be cut into strips and pulled through burlap can be hooked: new or recycled fabrics, yarns, foils, plastics, or fleece.

◀ *This hooked rug was made by Mennonites in Perth County, Ontario (measures 38 x 27in, c 1900).*

▼ *Hooked rug from Trois Riviéres, Québec. The rug includes a fringed border for decoration, (measures 38 x 24in, c1900).*

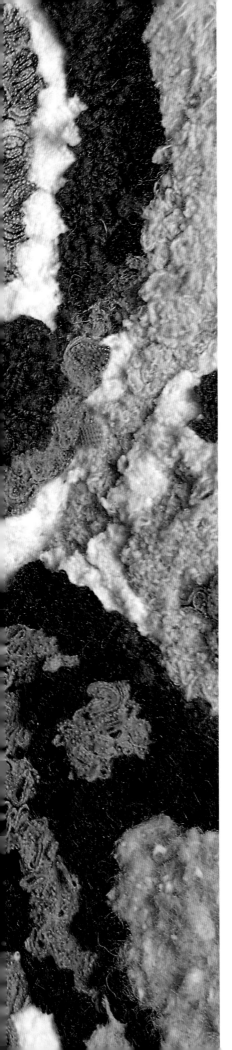

How to Hook

The rag strips stay in the burlap ground fabric because their thickness displaces the threads in the weave and the threads squeeze the loops in place. Using a frame to stretch the burlap taut will make the hooking faster and easier to manage but it is not strictly necessary.

1 Rug hooking is done with the right side of the work facing you. The hand that holds the hook is above the surface of the burlap. Beneath the burlap the thumb and forefinger of the other hand hold the cut strip, ready to guide it into the hook. Poke the hook through an opening in the weave of the burlap and grab the strip with the hook.

2 Pull the end of the strip up through the weave to the top of the burlap, so that at least ½ inch shows above the burlap.

3 Poke the hook back down through an opening in the weave of the burlap near to where the end of the strip comes through and pull a loop to the top of the burlap. A loop of between ¼ inch and ½ inch is standard for most hooking. Repeat the process by placing your hook near the loop that was just pulled up and poking through the burlap to draw up another loop.

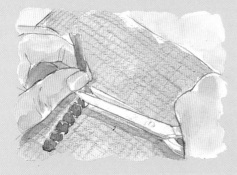

4 When ending your row of hooking, pull the remainder of the strip to the top surface. Trim the ends of the strip to match the rest of the pile height. Make sure you hook a pile dense enough to displace the threads in the weave of the burlap, otherwise the rag strips will pull out easily. Continue hooking until the burlap surface is covered.

◄ *Hooked rug (measures 29 x 46in).*

Fabrics with a pile, like velvet and corduroy, produce soft, slightly blurred loops while materials that reflect light, like satins or plastic bags, make clearly defined loops. Heavier fabrics such as those found in a wool blanket or coat make a thick 'primitive' style of rug; fine detailed work is best done in a silk blouse weight fabric. Printed fabrics make a spotted surface, while tweeds produce a variegated effect. Different fabrics may be combined in one rug or one type of fabric can be used throughout the rug.

Calculating Fabric Requirements

The amount of fabric needed to hook an area depends on the thickness of the fabric, the length of the pile and the density of the hooking. To get a rough idea of how much fabric a rug will require, work it out based on one of your own hooking samples.

1 Mark a square of 6 x 6 inches on your burlap. This gives you a quarter of a square foot. Cut out a square of hooking fabric 20 x 20 inches.

2 Hook the marked square of burlap. Cut the fabric into strips as you need them. If you need more fabric, cut a second 20 x 20 inches square.

◄ *Detail of* JONI *by Lizzie Reakes, showing a cut surface.*

▼ *Mat from Québec, hooked from cotton and wool fabric strips and yarns (measures 40 x 55in).*

3 When the square of burlap is completely hooked, make a note of the amount of fabric used. Multiply this number by four to discover how much fabric you require per square foot. Figure out the total number of square feet in your rug (a rug that is 3 x 5 feet is 15 square feet). Multiply the fabric requirements for one foot by the square footage of your rug to discover how much fabric you will need for the entire rug.

This calculation provides a guide but not a precise amount. Part of the charm of hooked rugs is their 'make-do' quality. If you do not have enough of one color of fabric to finish a rug, it might not matter. In many old rugs, when the maker ran out of one fabric she simply continued hooking in a similar fabric.

Another solution is to make a rug with small areas of different colors, such as the *Heart* or *Diamond* rug projects (pages 44 and 77). These are great for using up odd bits of fabric.

◀ Detail of FLYING GARDENER CHILDREN'S RUG *by Juju Vail. This detail shows how similar blue and green fabrics are used to make up 'solid' blue and green areas.*

▲ The maker of this old, hooked rug may have run out of fabric while hooking the border but carried on in another color (measures 23 x 63in).

Blending

Blending shades of similar colors together can also extend the quantity of recycled fabrics as well as providing livelier colors. I have done this in the black area of the *Flying Gardener* rug project. Small patches of a charcoal gray sweater mingle with sparkly black nylon and a black knit sweatshirt. This gave three times the quantity of recycled 'black' fabric and made a richer surface.

Blending fabrics can be achieved by simply hooking small, irregularly shaped areas of close colors next to each other. Another way to blend fabrics is to hook with two strips of fabric at once and then trim the pile so that both fabrics show. This technique can be used to fade one color into another.

Size of Rag

Fabric strips must fit through the holes in the weave of the burlap, but this is the only restriction. A very fine pile of ⅛ inch wide silk strips can be hooked by working on a monks cloth and using an extra fine hook, or a chunky primitive pile can be hooked from 2 inch wide tweeds on a burlap ground fabric.

To create an even pile out of different fabrics, thicker fabrics will need to be cut narrower than thin ones. However, it is possible that within the same rug you may create a detailed area using a thinner fabric then fill in the background in a thicker, faster to hook fabric.

The loops of thicker fabrics will be distorted if they are wider than the hole in the weave of the burlap. If the rag strips are not distorted in the hooking process, then clear loops will be obvious. The direction of the rug maker's hooking can be seen. This can be a feature of the rug's design, with loops in straight lines, swirly shapes or outlining motifs.

The Pile

A hooked rug's pile can be long and shaggy, short and neat, looped or cut. Most hooked rugs have a looped pile of about ½ inch high but there is no limit to the height. Rugs can include piles of different heights or make a feature of loops that are occasionally left longer.

The pile can be trimmed. This eliminates loops and makes a rug with a carpet-like surface. If the loops of the pile are to be cut, it is a good idea to pull them quite long, about 1 inch, so that they are easier to trim back. This can be a faster way to hook since you do not need to worry about the length of the pile as it will be even once it is trimmed. However, this method uses more fabric.

Adding Details to Hooking

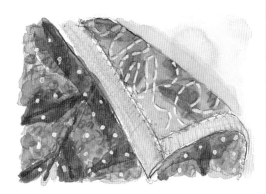

Sometimes a design may be enlivened with dots of color, one or two loops each, scattered over an area. An example would be snowfall in a winter scene. This can be done after the rest of the hooked surface is complete. Carry a long strip across the back of the rug, pulling it through the pile where needed. Long strips carried across the back are more vulnerable than ordinary hooking so it is best to coat the rug back with latex then line the rug.

▼ Blue Box
by Susan Lindsay
(measures 4½ x 5½in).

THE FLYING GARDENER CHILDREN'S RUG

HOOKED RUGS ARE IDEAL FOR DECORATING CHILDREN'S ROOMS. THE DIFFERENT TEXTURES GIVE LITTLE HANDS (AND FEET) SOMETHING TO EXPLORE, WHILE FAVORITE ANIMALS CAN BE EASILY INCLUDED. THIS RUG WAS DESIGNED FOR A LITTLE GIRL WHO LIKES CATS. THE DESIGN WAS MADE FROM A FABRIC COLLAGE. AND IS MULTI-DIRECTIONAL, SO THAT IT CAN BE PLACED IN THE CENTER OF A ROOM AND VIEWED FROM ANY DIRECTION.

YOU WILL NEED

- ≈ *1½ yards burlap for ground fabric*
- ≈ *1½ yards burlap for lining fabric*
- ≈ *an assortment of clothes, fabrics, and yarns*
- ≈ *a primitive size hook*
- ≈ *scissors*
- ≈ *ruler*
- ≈ *marker pens in three colors*
- ≈ *latex adhesive*
- ≈ *rug frame*
- ≈ *G-clamps (optional)*
- ≈ *trestles (optional)*

1 Draw a rectangle 44 x 30in on burlap ground fabric. Enlarge and transfer the design using a marker pen in one color to draw the grid on the burlap, another to draw the design, and a third to make corrections.

2 Allow for a border area of 3in. Mount the burlap on the hooking frame.

3 Begin by hooking the gardener. Add small amounts of red and yellow fabrics to her blue and green striped dress to enliven the composition.

4 To make the 'red' cat blend pink, orange, red and light brown fabrics. The yellow cat's stripes are made from a printed yellow and red fabric. His face is made from a paler yellow fabric so that it stands out.

BRIGHT IDEA

You will not be able to see the whole design on the frame at once. To help balance the elements of the design hook the motifs first then, when they look right, hook the background ≈

5 To make the flowers in the flower pot, pull long loops of a T-shirt fabric and leave them uncut. A novelty yarn has been hooked into the background around the flowers to give them sparkle.

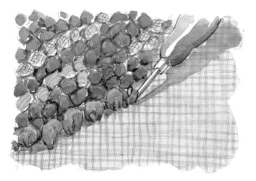

6 To give the rug movement and the impression of water pouring from the watering can, hook the green and purple backgrounds with a directional line.

38

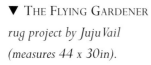

▼ THE FLYING GARDENER *rug project by Juju Vail (measures 44 x 30in).*

7 Remove the rug from the frame and lay it face down on a flat surface. Cut away any surplus burlap, leaving a border of 2in.

8 Place the lining piece of burlap on to the reverse of the rug. Use a marker pen to draw around the rug. Following the marked outline, cut the lining burlap.

9 Apply a thin layer of latex over the reverse of the rug and leave to dry for five minutes. Press down the hem allowance. At the corners, pinch the excess burlap and miter the edges, using small amounts of latex to stick them into shape. Recoat the hem with latex and allow to dry for three minutes.

10 Lay the burlap lining fabric on to the latexed reverse of the rug, press and smooth down so that the rug lies flat. Allow to dry overnight.

BRIGHT IDEA
To blend fabrics, hook with two different colored strips of fabric at once then trim the loops to expose a multi-colored pile ≈

HEN IN THE GARDEN RUG

Hens were a common motif on old, hooked rugs. Liz Kitching's *Hen in the Garden Rug* has updated this theme and made a rug that looks equally good in a period or modern home. The aged look of this rug is achieved by using heathery wool tweeds. Their muted colors look faded and aged, even when the fabrics are new.

1 Draw a rectangle 30 x 42in on the burlap. Enlarge and transfer the design using a marker pen in one color to draw the grid on the burlap, another to draw the design, and a third color to make corrections.

2 Allow for a border area of at least 3in. Mount the burlap on the hooking frame. Cut strips of assorted fabrics, including tweeds, approximately ½in wide. These will be hooked doubled over so that the loops of the pile are about ¼in

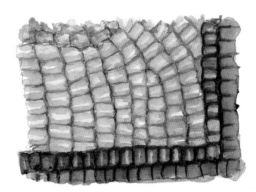

wide. Hook loops in parallel lines about ¼in apart, radiating from the motifs. The loops will be distinct and form a linear pattern in themselves.

You Will Need

≈ *1½ yards burlap for ground fabric*

≈ *1½ yards burlap for lining fabric*

≈ *an assortment of clothes, fabrics, and yarns, including a variety of wool tweeds*

≈ *a primitive size hook*

≈ *scissors*

≈ *ruler*

≈ *tape measure*

≈ *marker pens in three colors*

≈ *latex adhesive*

≈ *rug frame*

≈ *G-clamps (optional)*

≈ *trestles (optional)*

◀ Hen In The Garden rug project by Liz Kitching (measures 30 x 42in).

3 Begin by hooking the flower, stem, leaves, hen, and cross designs. Fill in the backgrounds as radiating lines from these shapes.

4 Remove the rug from the frame and lay it face down on a flat surface. Cut away any surplus burlap, leaving a border of 2in.

5 Place the lining piece of burlap on to the reverse of the rug. Use a marker pen to draw around the rug. Following the marked outline, cut out the lining burlap.

6 Apply a thin layer of latex over the reverse of the rug and leave to dry for five minutes. Press down the hem allowance. At the corners, pinch the excess burlap and miter the edges, using small amounts of latex to stick them into shape. Recoat the hem with latex and allow to dry for three minutes.

7 Lay the burlap lining fabric on to the latexed reverse of the rug, press and smooth down so that the rug lies flat. Allow to dry overnight.

BRIGHT IDEA

Use heathery tweeds to obtain the variegated colors of the border and hen background ≈

DRESS PIN

SUSAN LINDSAY MAKES HOOKED 'PICTURES' FROM FINE SILKS AND HER WORK FEATURES MEMORIES OF CHILDHOOD CLOTHING. THIS DRESS PIN COULD BE WORN AS A BROOCH OR FASTENED TO SOME CARD TO MAKE A GREETING CARD OR PICTURE FOR FRAMING.

YOU WILL NEED

≈ ¼ yard natural linen

≈ scrap of cotton fabric for lining

≈ lightweight silk or silk type fabrics

≈ ⅜in brooch pin

≈ embroidery hoop

≈ extra fine hook

≈ rotary cutter and cutting mat (optional)

≈ scissors

≈ ruler

≈ marker pen

≈ thread

≈ needle

1 Make a photocopy of the template of the dress design (shown actual size on page 118) and cut it out. Trace this on to the linen with a marker pen, drawing the dress details by hand. Stretch the linen taut in the embroidery hoop.

2 Cut the silk fabrics into strips approximately ¼in wide.

3 Hook the dress with the extra fine hook, using silks, in black, green, yellow, and pink.

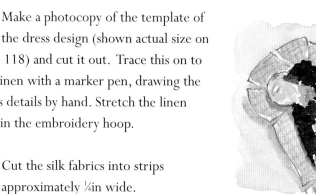

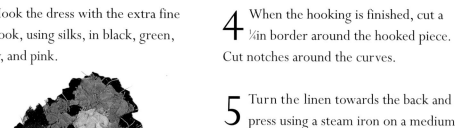

4 When the hooking is finished, cut a ¼in border around the hooked piece. Cut notches around the curves.

5 Turn the linen towards the back and press using a steam iron on a medium setting.

NOTE

The fabrics used to hook this pin are much thinner than an ordinary rug and therefore need a denser fabric than burlap. A linen has been used for this delightful project ≈

This design is so small that it can be hooked using an embroidery hoop to hold it taut ≈

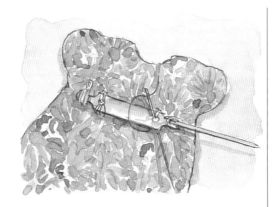

6 Place the dress pin on top of the cotton backing fabric. Cut out the cotton leaving a ¼in border.

7 Turn under the hem allowance and ladder stitch the lining to the hooked dress shape.

8 Center the pin, about ½in from the top, on the back. Stitch in place.

▼ *Hooked pins by Susan Lindsay.*

HEART RUG

HEARTS ARE A FAMILIAR FOLK ART MOTIF. THEY ARE EASILY DRAWN ON BURLAP AND HOOK UP QUICKLY. THE SQUARES IN THIS RUG BY AMANDA TOWNEND COULD BE REARRANGED TO MAKE A HALL RUNNER, EIGHT SQUARES HIGH BY TWO SQUARES WIDE. TO MAKE A DOOR MAT, THE RUG COULD BE REARRANGED AS THREE SQUARES WIDE BY TWO SQUARES HIGH.

YOU WILL NEED

- ≈ 1½ yards burlap for ground fabric
- ≈ 1½ yards burlap for lining fabric
- ≈ an assortment of clothes, fabrics, and yarns
- ≈ a primitive size hook
- ≈ scissors
- ≈ ruler
- ≈ tape measure
- ≈ marker pens in three colors
- ≈ latex adhesive
- ≈ rug frame
- ≈ G-clamps (optional)
- ≈ trestles (optional)

1 Draw a rectangle 36½ x 27in on the burlap. Divide the width and the length of the rug into four equal sections to make up the 16 squares. Make a template of the heart pattern and trace it in each square.

2 Allow for a border area of at least 3in. Mount the burlap on the hooking frame. Cut strips of rag approximately 1in wide from an assortment of wool, man-made, cotton, knitted, and woven fabrics.

3 Begin by hooking the hearts in fabrics and colors according to the pattern. Finish the rug by hooking the squares around the hearts. Use patterned fabrics to obtain variegated colors.

BRIGHT IDEA

This is a good rug for using up small quantities of leftover fabrics ≈

4 Remove the rug from the frame and lay it face down on a flat surface. Cut away surplus burlap, leaving a border of 2in all around.

5 Place the lining piece of burlap on to the reverse of the rug and use a marker pen to draw around the rug. Following the marked outline, cut out the lining burlap.

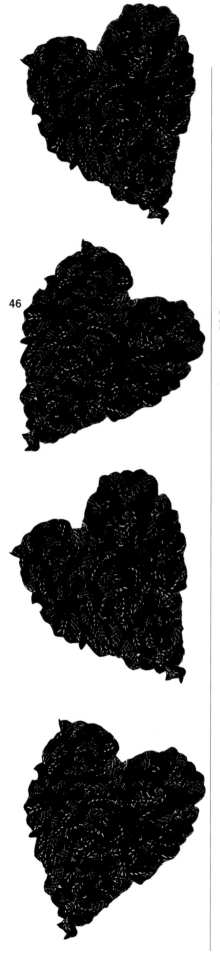

6 Apply a thin layer of latex over the reverse of the rug and leave to dry for five minutes. Press down the hem allowance. At the corners, pinch the excess burlap and miter the edges, using small amounts of latex to stick them into shape. Recoat the hem with latex and allow to dry for three minutes.

7 Lay the burlap lining fabric on to the latexed reverse of the rug, press and smooth down so that the rug lies flat. Allow to dry overnight

▼ HEART *hooked rug project by Amanda Townend (measures 36½ x 27in).*

GOLDEN HAMSTRINGS
RUNNER

LIZZIE REAKES' UNIQUE STYLE OF HOOKING GIVES HER RUGS A PAINTED LOOK. THE TOPS OF
THE LOOPS ARE CUT OFF, LEAVING A SHORT, DENSE PILE THAT RE-CREATES HER PAINTED DESIGNS
BEAUTIFULLY. THIS DESIGN CELEBRATES HER ENTHUSIASM FOR SOCCER AND ITS BOLD GRAPHIC
DESIGN WOULD COMPLEMENT A MODERN SETTING.

1 Draw a rectangle 65 x 28in on burlap
ground fabric. Enlarge and transfer
the design using a marker pen in one color
to draw the grid on the burlap, another to
draw the design, and a third color to make
corrections.

2 Allow for a border area of at least
3in. Mount the burlap on the hooking
frame. Cut the fabric into long strips,
approximately ⅛in wide.

3 Begin hooking in the center of the
rug, forming rows of close loops. As
you complete areas of about 3in square,
shear the tops off the loops to create a cut
pile surface. The pile should be about ¼in
in height after it is sheared. Continue
hooking and shearing until complete.

YOU WILL NEED

≈ 2 yards burlap for
  ground fabric

≈ 2 yards burlap for
  lining fabric

≈ as assortment of clothes,
  fabrics, and yarns

≈ a primitive size hook

≈ rotary cutter and
  cutting board (optional)

≈ scissors

≈ ruler

≈ tape measure

≈ marker pens in three
  colors

≈ latex adhesive

≈ rug frame

≈ G-clamps (optional)

≈ trestles (optional)

◄ GOLDEN HAMSTRINGS
hooked rug by Lizzie Reakes
(measures 65 x 28in).

4 Remove the rug from the frame and lay it face down on a flat surface. Cut away any surplus burlap, leaving a border of 2in.

5 Place the lining piece of burlap on to the reverse of the rug. Use a marker pen to draw around the rug. Following the marked outline, cut out the lining burlap.

6 Apply a thin layer of latex over the reverse of the rug and leave to dry for five minutes. Press down the hem allowance. At the corners, pinch the excess burlap and miter the edges, using small amounts of latex to stick them into shape. Recoat the hem with latex and allow to dry for three minutes.

7 Lay the burlap lining fabric on to the latexed reverse of the rug, press and smooth down. Cut off any excess burlap so that the rug lies flat. Allow to dry overnight.

NOTE
Don't work too much of the rug before you shear the pile or it will be hard to cut ≈

"THERE WAS NOTHING ON IT BUT TEA" PICTURE

THIS WALL HANGING WAS DESIGNED FOR A 'TEAPOTS' EXHIBITION. IT WAS INSPIRED BY THE MAD HATTER'S TEA PARTY IN *ALICE IN WONDERLAND* BY LEWIS CARROLL. LYNNE STEIN USES A VARIETY OF YARNS IN HER DESIGNS TO BUILD UP AREAS OF DETAIL AND CREATE UNUSUAL TEXTURES.

YOU WILL NEED

≈ *1 yard monks cloth for ground fabric*

≈ *1 yard cotton cloth for lining fabric*

≈ *an assortment of clothes, fabrics, and yarns, including novelty yarns*

≈ *a primitive size hook*

≈ *an extra fine hook (optional)*

≈ *scissors*

≈ *ruler*

≈ *tape measure*

≈ *marker pens in three colors*

≈ *latex adhesive*

≈ *rug frame*

≈ *G-clamps (optional)*

≈ *trestles (optional)*

1 Draw a rectangle 24 x 26in on the burlap. Enlarge and transfer the design using a marker pen in one color to draw the grid on to the burlap, another to draw the design, and a third color to make corrections.

2 Allow for a border area of at least 3in. Mount the monks cloth on the hooking frame.

3 Start by hooking the outline of the teapot, using strips cut from black tights or T-shirt fabric. Hook the blue lines on the teapot in a combination of novelty yarns and fabric strips. The flower motifs are hooked solely with yarns, including some glittery metallics, to add sparkle.

BRIGHT IDEA

An extra fine hooking needle will make it easier to hook with yarns and thin fabrics ≈

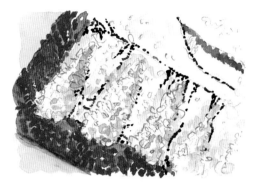

4 When hooking areas like the floral crêpe curtains above the teapot, and the folds and undulations of the table-cloth underneath, leave some of the loops longer so that they can be trimmed, sculpted with sharp scissors, or deliberately left longer to create sculptural relief areas. Some gold yarns should be incorporated in the hooking to provide a shimmery effect.

5 The teapot should be hooked using a combination of cream and white fabrics and yarns, including cottons, silk, polyester, and linen.

6 Hook the background area in a combination of cream and white fabrics and yarns, including net, nylon, mohair, bouclé, and other novelty yarns, to give it a softer, more textural appearance than the teapot itself. The direction of your hooking should be in contrast to that of the teapot.

▲ THERE WAS NOTHING ON IT BUT TEA *hooked project by Lynne Stein (measures 24 x 24in).*

7 Black lines can be hooked using three or four strands of black yarn. To make sensitive, fine lines, hook long loops then, when the pile around them is complete, trim back the long loops.

8 The silver spiral shape should be hooked in silver lurex/metallic polyester, using a comparatively broader fabric strip, (approximately ¼in) to give it extra boldness.

9 The red frame around the design is hooked in a variety of red fabrics and yarns, using different hooking directions to distinguish it from the rest of the hooking.

10 The picture includes hand-embroidered tabs which display fragments of the title. One end of each of the embroidered tabs is poked through the design at an appropriate place along the inside edge of the red frame, and draped diagonally to the outer edge of the frame where it is poked through again so that the ends are on the wrong side of the hooking. These are then stitched into place on the wrong side.

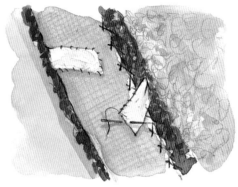

11 When the hooking is complete and you have checked that the density of the pile is fairly even, remove the rug from the frame. Cut away the surplus monks cloth, leaving a border of 2in.

12 Apply a thin layer of latex over the reverse of the rug. Leave to dry for five minutes. Press down the hem allowance. At the four corners, pinch the excess burlap and miter the edges, using small amounts of latex to stick the corners into shape. Allow to dry overnight.

13 Place the rug on your lining fabric and cut round it leaving 2in beyond the edge of the rug. Turn under the hem of the lining fabric and pin. Ladder stitch the lining fabric in place.

HOOKED HAT 🌱

THIS HOOKED HAT IS REMARKABLY WARM AND WATER RESISTANT. IT WITHSTANDS FOLDING AND BATTERING. THE HOOKED BAND IS EDGED WITH STRIPED SILK PIPING, AND COMPLETED WITH A QUILTED, SLASHED SILK AND FELT TOP. BEADED DECORATION AND A SILK LINING ADD DELIGHTFUL FINISHING TOUCHES.

YOU WILL NEED

- ≈ ½ yard burlap for hooking ground fabric
- ≈ an assortment of fabrics, and yarns
- ≈ ½ yard striped fabric for piping cover
- ≈ ½ yard lining fabric
- ≈ ½ yard felt for hat top
- ≈ ½ yard silk fabric for hat top
- ≈ 1½ yards thick piping
- ≈ a primitive size hook
- ≈ scissors
- ≈ rotary cutter and mat
- ≈ ruler
- ≈ thread and needle
- ≈ marker pens in three colors
- ≈ latex adhesive
- ≈ sewing machine
- ≈ rug frame
- ≈ G-clamps (optional)
- ≈ trestles (optional)

1 Measure your head circumference just above the ear and add 2in – this will give you the length of your hat band. The height of the hat band is 3in. Mark the hat band on burlap.

2 Enlarge and transfer the design using a marker pen in one color to draw the grid on the burlap, another to draw the design, and a third color to make corrections.

3 To make the piping case cut two pieces of the striped fabric across the diagonal of the fabric. These strips should be the length of the hat band plus 1¼in for the seam allowance, by 2½in wide.

4 Stitch the piping case, raw edges together and wrong sides facing, leaving a ¼in seam allowance. Attach a safety pin to one end of the piping and pull it through the piping case.

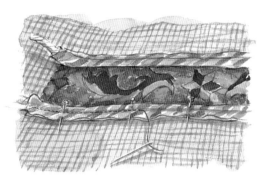

5 Allow for a border area of at least 3in. Mount the burlap on the hooking frame. Hand stitch the piping to the burlap, following the seam of the piping along the edge of the hat band. The raw edges of the piping should be outside the hat band. Repeat this so that the top and bottom of the hat band has piped edges.

6 Select your fabrics and cut them into strips. Hook the motifs, then hook the background to the piping edge.

7 Take the burlap off the frame. Cut out the hat, leaving a 1½in seam allowance all around.

8 Spread latex on the wrong side of the hat band. Wait five minutes and then fold back the hem and piping seam allowance, sticking them to the latex. Leave the center back seam allowance free so that you can stitch the back seam.

9 Slip stitch the piping together at the center back, concealing the seam allowance. Slip stitch the center back seam together. Stick the back seam allowance to the hat band with latex.

> **NOTE**
>
> The wavy machine stitching is for decoration and to stop the silk from fraying beyond the stitching lines. If your sewing machine does not have a wavy stitch setting, use a zig-zag stitch set on a long stitch length instead ≈

▼*Hooked and embroidered hat by Juju Vail.*

10 Make a pattern for the top of the hat by calculating the radius and adding a ¼in seam allowance. The radius is equal to the length of the hat band plus ¾in ease, divided by 6.3. Once you have found the radius, use a measuring tape to make a circle by placing a pin in the end, holding a pencil at the desired length and drawing a circle on the silk and on the felt. Cut out the silk and felt circles.

11 Machine embroider the felt and silk tops together with parallel rows of wavy machine stitching, 1½in apart. Stitch 1½in apart parallel lines at a right angle to the first set. Slash diagonal lines in the silk from one corner to the next of each square. Sew beads at the intersection of each set of four slashes.

12 Ladder stitch the hat top to the piping, turning under the seam allowance as you stitch.

13 Cut a lining band and top to the same measurements as the hat band and top. Stitch the center back seam and stitch the top in place, easing in any extra fabric.

14 Use a ladder stitch to hold the lining in place, turning under the seam allowance as you go.

BRIGHT IDEA

If the stitching or any of the burlap shows on the right side of the center back seam, hide it by stitching pile from each side of the seam together, concealing any exposed burlap ≈

COTTAGE GARDEN RUG

This charming rug by Liz Kitching features simple flowers. A checked black and white fabric has been used to create the variegated 'gray' background. Look for old coats and suits at second-hand stores to find the unusual and colorful tweed fabrics that Liz Kitching favors.

You Will Need

≈ 1½ yards burlap for ground fabric

≈ 1½ yards burlap for lining fabric

≈ an assortment of clothes and fabrics, including a variety of wool tweeds

≈ a primitive size hook

≈ scissors

≈ ruler

≈ tape measure

≈ marker pens in three colors

≈ latex adhesive

≈ rug frame

≈ G-clamps (optional)

≈ trestles (optional)

1 Draw a rectangle 42 x 39in on burlap ground fabric. Enlarge and transfer the design using a marker pen in one color to draw the grid on the burlap, another to draw the design, and a third color to make corrections.

2 Allow for a border area of at least 3in. Mount the burlap on the hooking frame. Cut strips of rag and tweed fabrics approximately ½in wide. These will be hooked doubled over so that the loops of the pile are about ¼in wide. Hook loops in parallel lines about ¼in apart, radiating from the motifs. The loops will be distinct and form a linear pattern in themselves.

NOTE

If you are using garments, prepare them by cutting off the seams, opening any hems, removing buttons, zippers, or any other trim. This will create large pieces of fabric from which to cut your strips ≈

3 Begin hooking the flower, stem, leaves, hen, and blocked-in areas. Fill in the background by outlining one row at a time until you have built up the full rug. Use heathery tweeds to obtain the variegated colors.

4 Remove the rug from the frame and lay it face down on a flat surface. Cut away any surplus burlap, leaving a border of 2in.

▼ COTTAGE GARDEN
hooked rug project
by Liz Kitching
(measures 30 x 39in).

5 Place the lining piece of burlap on to the reverse of the rug. Use a marker pen to draw around the rug. Following the marked outline, cut out the lining burlap.

6 Apply a thin layer of latex over the reverse of the rug and leave to dry for five minutes. Press down the hem allowance. At the corners, pinch the excess burlap and miter the edges, using small amounts of latex to stick them into shape. Recoat the hem with latex and allow to dry for three minutes.

7 Lay the burlap lining fabric on to the latexed reverse of the rug, press, and smooth down. Cut off any excess burlap so that the rug lies flat. Allow to dry overnight.

WHALE RUG

Rug hooking was a popular pastime in maritime American and British communities, where boat, fish, and whale themes abound. Jan Tricker has updated this theme by expanding the size of the whale and using bright, vibrant colors. Somber wools and tweeds could be substituted for the bright fabrics to make a hooked rug for a period home.

1 Draw a rectangle 59 x 35⅓in on the burlap. Enlarge and transfer the design using a marker pen in one color to draw the grid on the burlap, another to draw the design, and a third color to make corrections. Allow for a border area of at least 3in. Mount the burlap on the hooking frame.

2 Cut all your chosen fabric into long 1in wide strips. Begin by hooking the whale motif, using warm vibrant colors to work the design.

3 Hook the background in various shades of blue. For the impression of water, hook one long strip of fabric into a curving shape. Then hook a parallel line in another strip of fabric so the wave is built up in radiating wavy lines.

You Will Need

- ≈ 2 yards burlap for ground fabric
- ≈ 2 yards burlap for lining fabric
- ≈ an assortment of clothes, fabrics, and yarns
- ≈ a primitive size hook
- ≈ scissors
- ≈ ruler
- ≈ tape measure
- ≈ marker pens in three colors
- ≈ latex adhesive
- ≈ rug frame
- ≈ G-clamps (optional)
- ≈ trestles (optional)

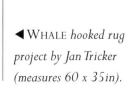

◀ WHALE *hooked rug project by Jan Tricker (measures 60 x 35in).*

4 Remove the rug from the frame and lay it face down on a flat surface. Cut away surplus burlap, leaving a border of 2in.

5 Place the lining piece of burlap on to the reverse of the rug. Use a marker pen to draw around the rug. Following the marked outline, cut out the lining burlap.

BRIGHT IDEA

Choose a fabric with a small pattern to get flecked areas of color as in the curved wedge shapes on the whale's belly ≈

6 Apply a thin layer of latex over the reverse of the rug. Leave to dry for five minutes. Press down the hem allowance. At the corners, pinch the excess burlap and miter the edges, using a little latex to stick them into shape. Recoat the hem with latex and allow to dry for three minutes.

7 Lay the burlap lining fabric on to the latexed reverse of the rug, press, and smooth down so that the rug lies flat. Allow to dry overnight.

SMALL SCALLOPED RUG

THIS RUG WAS INSPIRED BY THE SCALLOPS USED TO EDGE OLD HOOKED AND APPLIQUÉD RUGS. THE DESIGN GAVE ME A CHANCE TO DISPLAY THE PATTERNS OF SOME OF THE FABRICS AND CLOTHING I HAVE COLLECTED OVER THE YEARS. IT WAS MADE TO DECORATE THE FLOOR OF A VERY SMALL TOILET BUT IT WOULD BE EQUALLY SUITABLE IN A PANTRY OR ON THE THRESHOLD OF A DOOR.

SMALL SCALLOPED RUG

YOU WILL NEED

≈ ¾ yard burlap for ground fabric

≈ ¾ yard cotton cloth for lining fabric

≈ an assortment of clothes, fabrics, and yarns for hooking

≈ an assortment of fabric scraps for making scallops

≈ a primitive size hook

≈ scissors

≈ tailor's chalk

≈ marker pens in three colors

≈ latex adhesive

≈ sewing machine

≈ needle and thread

≈ furry novelty yarn

≈ rotary cutter and mat

≈ rug frame

≈ G-clamps (optional)

≈ trestles (optional)

1 Enlarge and transfer the hooking design using a marker pen in one color to draw the grid on the burlap, another to draw the design, and a third color to make corrections.

2 Make a template for the scallops. The scallops in the first row are 3½in wide and 3in high. For the second row of scallops repeat this procedure, making the scallops 3½in wide and 4in high. Add a ½in seam allowance around all sides of the scallop template.

BRIGHT IDEA

To make a scallop template draw a rectangle on a piece of paper, the height and width of the scallop. Make a crease in the paper, marking half the width of the rectangle. Draw a curve from where the crease meets the top of the rectangle to half way up one side. Fold the paper along the crease and cut out the scallop template, following the curved line and the rectangle parameters ≈

---

3 Using the scallop templates, cut 19 pairs of small scallops and 17 pairs of large ones from a variety of fabrics.

4 To make the scallops, put the fabric right sides together and stitch, leaving ½in seam allowance all around and the bottom end open. Clip and trim the seam allowance. Turn the scallops right side out and press.

5 Pin the smaller scallops in place first, with the raw edge ½in over the rug edge. Overlap the scallops slightly around the curve so that there are no gaps. Stitch the small scallops to the burlap. Center the larger scallops between the smaller scallops and stitch in place.

6 Allow for a border area of at least 3in. Mount the burlap on the hooking frame. Cut strips from the fabrics, clothing, and yarns.

▶ SMALL SCALLOPED RUG
project by Juju Vail
(measures 27 x 21in).

7 Hook the motifs first. Then hook the red backgrounds from several different shades of red, blending small amounts of yellow to make a red-orange color.

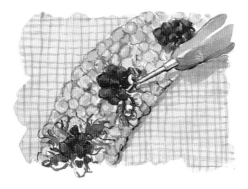

8 Hook the red polka dots and the yellow background. When this is finished, go back and hook the novelty yarn, leaving long loops to create a hairy effect around the polka dots.

9 Make the purple and green checks by blending fabrics. To blend fabrics, hook with two different colored strips at once, pulling long loops then trimming them to match the pile height. Hook right up to the scalloped edge.

10 Remove the rug from the frame and lay it face down on a flat surface. Cut away any surplus burlap, leaving a border of 2in. Clip the border so that it will curve when it is folded under the rug.

11 Place the lining fabric on to the reverse of the rug. Use tailor's chalk to draw around the hooked area of the rug. Add a 1in hem allowance to the lining and cut out.

12 Apply a thin layer of latex to the hooking on the reverse of the rug and leave to dry for five minutes. Then press the burlap hem back to the latex, adding more latex if necessary to stick down. Allow to dry overnight.

13 Ladder stitch the lining to the hooked rug back, concealing the scallop edges and turning under 1in hem allowance on the lining.

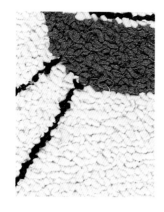

COAT ON A LINE PICTURE

THIS HOOKED PICTURE BY SUSAN LINDSAY COULD BE MOUNTED IN A BOX FRAME OR HUNG ON THE WALL AS IT IS. TO MOUNT A HOOKED PICTURE DIRECTLY ON THE WALL, TACK ONE SIDE OF A WIDE VELCRO STRIP ACROSS THE BACK OF THE PICTURE AND THEN MOUNT THE OTHER HALF OF THE VELCO STRIP TO A WOOD BATTEN OF EQUAL LENGTH. SCREW THE WOOD BATTEN TO THE WALL AND THEN ADHERE THE HOOKED PICTURE.

YOU WILL NEED

≈ *1 yard monks cloth for ground fabric*

≈ *1 yard cotton cloth for lining*

≈ *approximately 1½ yards or one large white woolen garment*

≈ *approximately ½ yard or one small black woolen garment*

≈ *approximately ½ yard or one small gray woolen garment*

≈ *a primitive size hook*

≈ *scissors*

≈ *marker pens in three colors*

≈ *latex adhesive*

≈ *1 yard twill tape*

≈ *needle and thread*

≈ *rug frame*

≈ *G-clamps (optional)*

≈ *trestles (optional)*

1 Draw a rectangle 27 x 27in on the monks cloth. Enlarge and transfer the design using a marker pen in one color to draw the grid on the monks cloth, another to draw the design, and a third color to make corrections. Allow for a border area of at least 3in. Mount the monks cloth on the hooking frame.

2 Lay the fabric on the cutting mat and cut it into strips of approximately ½in wide for lighter weight wools (dresses or light sweaters) and ⅝in wide for heavier weight wools (coats and jackets).

3 Begin by hooking a line of black border around the checks, coat, and washing line.

BRIGHT IDEA

If you can't find enough of one white woolen garment to make this picture, blend two whites together. Hook small areas of color next to each other or hook the white checks in a different white than that used for the main part of the rug ≈

4 Use the gray woolen fabric to fill in alternate blocks of the checked border and the buttons, collar, and cuffs of the coat.

5 Hook all the remaining areas in the white fabric.

6 Remove the rug from the frame. Cut away the surplus monks cloth, leaving a hem allowance of 2in. Herringbone stitch the hem allowance to the wrong side of the rug.

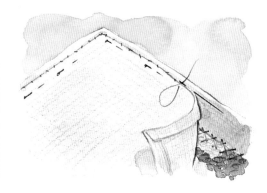

> **NOTE**
>
> Monks cloth is a harder wearing base fabric than burlap. It does not need to be backed with a latex adhesive application ≈

7 Place the lining fabric on to the reverse of the rug. Use a marker pen to draw around the rug. Following the marked outline, cut the lining fabric along the marked line.

8 Place the lining on the reverse of the rug and cover the edge with twill tape. Pin the twill tape in place, folding the corners to change direction. Ladder stitch both sides of the tape to the rug back.

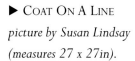

▶ COAT ON A LINE
*picture by Susan Lindsay
(measures 27 x 27in).*

ANGEL BENCH CUSHION

This cushion cover is made for a children's small bench. The angel, feather, and six-point star are common folk art motifs. They could be recombined in many different ways to achieve a variety of hooking patterns. This design would look wonderful hooked in vibrant colors against a black background.

1 Draw a rectangle the size of the finished cushion on the burlap. Enlarge and transfer the design using a marker pen in one color to draw the grid on the burlap, another to draw the design, and a third color to make corrections. Allow for a border area of at least 3in.

2 To make the piping case cut 2½in wide strips of a striped fabric. Piece together the lengths of striped fabric until you have enough to go all the way around the outside edge of the cushion – for this cushion a finished length of 71in was required.

3 Stitch the raw edges of the piping case together with wrong sides facing, leaving a ¼in seam allowance. Attach a safety pin to one end of the piping and pull it through the piping case.

You Will Need

- ≈ ½ yard burlap for ground fabric
- ≈ ½ yard burlap for lining fabric
- ≈ an assortment of clothes, fabrics, and yarns
- ≈ 1 yard striped fabric
- ≈ ½ yard silk fabric
- ≈ 2 yards thick piping
- ≈ ¾ yard 2in-thick foam
- ≈ a primitive size hook
- ≈ scissors
- ≈ needle and thread
- ≈ pins
- ≈ sewing machine
- ≈ ruler
- ≈ marker pens in three colors
- ≈ latex adhesive
- ≈ rug frame
- ≈ G-clamps (optional)
- ≈ trestles (optional)

4 Mount the burlap on the hooking frame. Hand stitch the piping to the burlap with the raw edge of the piping extending beyond the cushion. Trim the ends of the piping, turn under the raw edges, and slip stitch in place so that the piping makes a complete circle around the cushion cover.

5 Select a variety of fabrics and cut them into strips. Begin by hooking the motifs. Blend pink into the angel's cheeks and wings by hooking with a pale pink fabric and a white fabric at the same time, then cutting the pile. Use a pale blue or violet for the shadows of the angel's face and wings.

6 Hook the background right up to the piping edge.

7 Remove the pillow from the frame and lay it face down on a flat surface. Cut away surplus burlap, leaving a border of 2in.

8 Apply a thin layer of latex over the reverse of the cushion cover and leave to dry for five minutes. Press down the hem and piping seam allowance. Allow to dry overnight.

9 Cut two pieces of lining, the width of the cushion by three quarters of the length plus ¼in seam allowance all around. This gives measurements of 15 x 19in for this cushion. Turn under one of the 15in edges on each piece and machine stitch the hem in place.

10 Stitch the lining to the piping using ladder stitch, turning under the seam allowance and overlapping the two pieces in the middle so that the cushion back forms an envelope opening.

11 Cut the foam to the size of the cushion and insert it in place.

▼ ANGEL BENCH CUSHION *hooked project by Juju Vail (measures 21 x 15½in).*

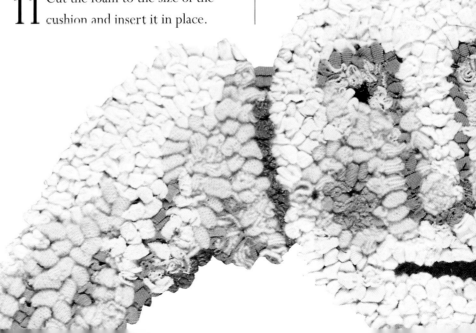

NEO-CLASSICAL RUG

THIS WALL HANGING BY LYNNE STEIN (MADE WITH THE ASSISTANCE OF ANGELA SMITH) WAS INSPIRED BY THE FABRIC AND WALLPAPER DESIGNS OF TIMNEY FOWLER. ALTHOUGH THE PALETTE OF THIS RUG IS LIMITED, THE VARIETY OF TEXTURES MAKE A RICH EFFECT. PRINTED, CHECKED, AND PLAID FABRICS IN BLACK, WHITE, AND GRAY CONTRIBUTE TO THE TEXTURAL EFFECT CREATED THROUGH UNUSUAL COMBINATIONS OF YARNS AND FABRICS.

YOU WILL NEED

≈ *1½ yards monks cloth for ground fabric*

≈ *1½ yards for rug lining*

≈ *an assortment of clothes, fabrics, and yarns, including novelty yarns*

≈ *a primitive size hook*

≈ *an extra fine hook (optional)*

≈ *scissors*

≈ *ruler*

≈ *tape measure*

≈ *marker pens in three colors*

≈ *latex adhesive*

≈ *rug frame*

≈ *G-clamps (optional)*

≈ *trestles (optional)*

1 Draw a rectangle 50 x 30in on to the monks cloth. Enlarge and transfer the design using a marker pen in one color to draw the grid on the cloth, another to draw the design, and a third color to make corrections. Allow for a border area of at least 3in. Mount the rug design on a hooking frame.

2 Hook the blackest areas with a combination of black fabrics and yarns, such as chenille and other novelty yarns, ribbon, cotton, tights, T-shirt, sweatshirts, and polyester knits.

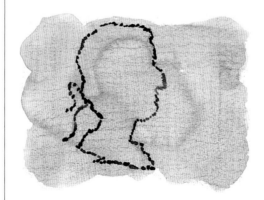

3 Outline the large head in a black nylon ribbon. Blend different black and gray fabrics and yarns within the head, including printed and checked fabrics.

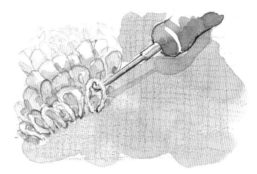

4 To make the 'white' background use a range of cream and white fabrics and yarns with very different textures. This rug includes furnishing fabrics, polyester, wool, net, linen, silk, and cotton. Use both smooth and fraying fabrics, and fuzzy yarns such as mohair. A range of different shades of gold, copper, and metallic threads and fabrics are included in the background to give it sparkle and richness.

NOTE
An extra fine hook will make hooking with yarns much easier ≈

▼ NEO-CLASSICAL PIECE
hooked rug project
by Lynne Stein
(measures 50 x 30in).

5 When the hooking is complete, and you have checked that the density of the pile is fairly even, remove the rug from the frame. Cut away the surplus monks cloth, leaving a border of 2in.

6 Apply a thin layer of latex over the reverse of the rug and leave to dry for five minutes. Press down the hem allowance, mitering the corners, and allow to dry overnight.

7 Place the rug on your lining fabric and cut around it, leaving 2in beyond the edge of the rug. Turn under the hem of the lining fabric and pin, then ladder stitch in place.

DIAMOND RUG

THE DIAMOND MOTIF IS OFTEN FEATURED IN OLD RAG RUGS. TRADITIONAL RUGS FEATURED A LARGE DIAMOND AS A CENTRAL MOTIF. LU MASON'S RUG REPEATS A DIAMOND SHAPE IN RICH SHADES OF BROWN AND BEIGE. THIS IS A GREAT PATTERN FOR USING UP OLD SCRAPS OF FABRIC AND IS SIMPLE TO ACHIEVE.

1 Draw a rectangle 5 x 3 feet on the burlap. Transfer the diamond pattern, using a wide ruler to achieve equidistant lines. Allow for a border area of at least 3in. Mount the burlap on the hooking frame.

2 Select a range of woolen fabrics in shades of beige, brown, and jewel colors. Cut these into strips of various lengths about 1in wide.

BRIGHT IDEA

Try to keep a balance of colors over the whole of the rug, so that one area does not seem too red while another area is too blue ≈

YOU WILL NEED

≈ *2 yards burlap for ground fabric*

≈ *2 yards burlap for lining fabric*

≈ *an assortment of clothes, fabrics, and yarns*

≈ *a primitive size hook*

≈ *scissors*

≈ *ruler*

≈ *tape measure*

≈ *marker pens in three colors*

≈ *latex adhesive*

≈ *rug frame*

≈ *G-clamps (optional)*

≈ *trestles (optional)*

◀ DIAMONDS EVERYWHERE *hooked rug project by Lu Mason (measures 60 x 36in).*

3 Begin by hooking the diagonal lines with fabric strips in shades of beige and brown. Different shades of these colors are used to make up each diagonal line. The similarity in tone and the contrast to the brighter, jewel colors of the rest of the rug make the pattern clearly visible.

4 Fill in each diamond with three blocks of color, working from the outside inward.

5 Remove the rug from the frame and lay it face down on a flat surface. Cut away any surplus burlap, leaving a border of 2in.

6 Place the lining piece of burlap on to the reverse of the rug. Use a marker pen to draw around the rug. Following the marked outline, cut out the lining burlap.

7 Apply a thin layer of latex over the reverse of the rug and leave to dry for five minutes. Press down the hem allowance. At the corners, pinch the excess burlap and miter the edges, using small amounts of latex to stick them into shape. Recoat the hem with latex and allow to dry for three minutes.

8 Lay the burlap lining fabric on to the latexed reverse of the rug, press, and smooth down so that the rug lies flat. Allow to dry overnight.

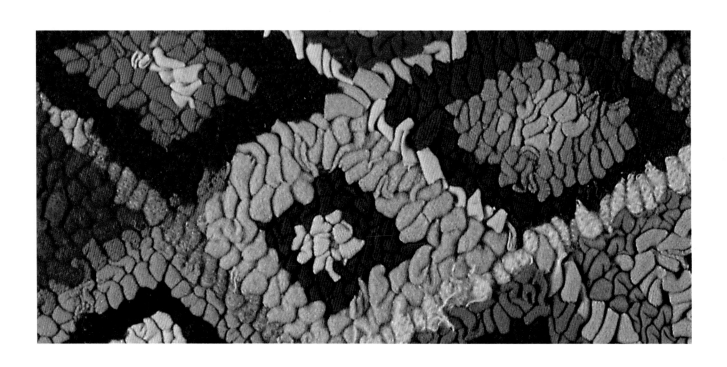

PRODDED RAG RUGS

▼ PORTRAIT #1. *It is difficult to tell from looking at a detail of Ben Hall's rug (previous page) that it is part of a man's face. But when the rug is viewed from a distance, the different colors of rag blend optically to make a portrait (measures 19 x 23in).*

Prodded rugs are made by poking strips of fabric through a burlap ground fabric. They have a long, shaggy pile, which blurs their design. They were often made for more utilitarian use than hooked rugs. Their long pile hides dirt well and so they were put into service rather than saved for the parlor. Few good examples of old prodded rugs exist since they were so well used.

A common design for a prodded mat was one large, diamond motif touching the center of each edge of a rectangular mat. The diamond was then prodded with smaller diamond motifs inside.

▲ HEAD OF A GLADIATOR. *Prodded wall hanging by Ben Hall (measures 17 x 21in).*

The long, shaggy pile of prodded rugs makes details difficult to distinguish. Large, simple designs are best suited to this technique. However, the shaggy pile can be an advantage when it is used to blend the colors optically, like pointillist paintings. Generally speaking prodded rugs use short fabric strips, each of which only goes through the burlap once to produce two strands of the rug. Therefore the prodded rug lends itself well to designs with frequent color changes. This can be very effective when several colors are prodded near to each other so that they blend optically to form an area of one color.

The choice of fabrics, size of rag, and length of pile are as limitless for prodded rugs as they are for hooked rugs.

▶ PORTRAIT #2. *This prodded portrait rug by Ben Hall was inspired by a self-portrait of Cézanne (measures 18 x 25in).*

HOW TO MAKE A PRODDED RUG

To prod a rug, the burlap must be stretched taut on a frame. Prodded rugs are worked with the wrong side of the rug facing you.

1 Using a prodding tool, force a small hole in between the weave of the burlap.

2 Push through one end of a strip of fabric about 1in wide by 3½in long.

3 Move along about ¼in and make another opening in the weave of the burlap. Push through the other end of the fabric strip using both hands, one on each side of the rug. Pull the ends of the strip until they are even in length, about 1½in.

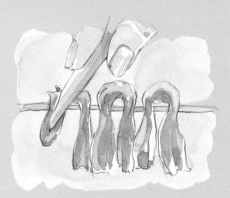

4 Prod a second strip of fabric through the rug in the same way about ¼in from the last one. Continue prodding until the surface of the rug is covered and no burlap can be seen on the right side of the rug. When the prodding is complete, check the pile to be sure that it is even and trim any long ends.

◀ PRODDED RUNNER
by Amanda Townend.

◀ CONE *prodded wall
hanging by Ben Hall
(measures 22½ x 18in).*

▼ *This beautiful old mat
displays a bull's eye star
design. It is typical of the
simple geometric designs
that were common among
prodded rugs (measures
26½ x 38in).*

MOONLIT FOREST RUG

THIS RUG WAS INSPIRED BY A FOREST NEAR ANITA LANGHAM'S HOME IN NORTHEAST ENGLAND. THE FOREST HILLS ARE BATHED IN MOONLIGHT AND SHADOWS. THIS IS A VERY LARGE RUG AND MAKING IT CAN CONSUME A LOT OF FABRIC. ANITA'S FAMILY SAW SOME OF THEIR FAVORITE CLOTHES AND BLANKETS DISAPPEAR AS THE RUG GREW.

YOU WILL NEED

- ≈ 2 yards burlap for ground fabric
- ≈ 2 yards burlap for lining fabric
- ≈ an assortment of clothes and fabrics
- ≈ a prodding tool
- ≈ scissors
- ≈ ruler
- ≈ tape measure
- ≈ rotary cutter and cutting mat
- ≈ marker pens in three colors
- ≈ latex adhesive
- ≈ rug frame
- ≈ G-clamps
- ≈ trestles

1 Draw a rectangle 74 x 46in on the burlap. Enlarge and transfer the design using a marker pen in one color to draw the grid on the burlap, another to draw the design, and a third color to make corrections. Allow for a border area of at least 3in. Mount the burlap on the hooking frame.

2 Choose a selection of appropriate fabrics, such as dense cottons or woven wools. Cut these into strips, parallel to the grain of the fabric about 1 x 3½in.

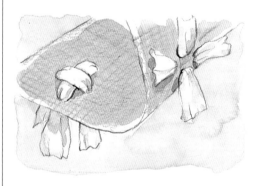

3 Begin by making the moon and the stars. Each star is made up of a cross section of strips.

4 Make the trunks of the trees by tapering from two strip widths to one and use tweedy fabrics to look like bark.

5 Form the tree foliage, adding bits of trunk fabric to make it look as if branches are peeping through the foliage.

6 Outline the triangle border, then fill it in with gold colored fabrics.

7 Make the night sky around the moon and stars using shades of inky navy, black, and charcoal.

BRIGHT IDEAS

To make the trees in the background recede, prod them in darker colors than those that are in the foreground of the design ≈

To obtain the rich golds used in this rug, boil ten pints of water and add a bag of old onion skins. Add pale blue blankets to this solution. The blue will dye to a gold color. Rinse the blankets in cool water and dry ≈

8 To create the hills, follow the curve of the horizon around the night sky, working bands of colors that shade from very pale olive, through medium olive, moss green, khaki, tan, chestnut, dark chocolate, deep purple, and indigo to the black at the edge of the rug.

▼ MOONLIT FOREST
*prodded rug project by Anita Langham
(measures 74 x 45½in).*

9 When the prodding is complete, remove the rug from the frame and lay it face down on a flat surface. Cut away any surplus burlap, leaving a border of 2in.

10 Place the lining piece of burlap on to the reverse of the rug. Use a marker pen to draw around the rug. Following the marked outline, cut out the lining burlap.

11 Apply a thin layer of latex over the reverse of the rug and leave to dry for five minutes. Press down the hem allowance. At the corners, pinch the excess burlap and miter the edges, using small amounts of latex to stick them into shape. Recoat the hem with latex and allow to dry for three minutes.

12 Lay the burlap lining fabric on to the latexed reverse of the rug, press, and smooth down so that the rug lies flat. Allow to dry overnight. Trim the rug pile so that it is of an even height.

FIRE RUG

THIS PRODDED RUG BY BEN HALL HAS A DEEP, SHAGGY PILE. IT IS PRODDED IN RICH, SOLID
COLORS OF DENSE COTTONS AND WOVEN WOOLS. THE GEOMETRIC DESIGN IS EASY TO FOLLOW
AND IDEAL FOR A PRODDED RUG.

1 Draw a rectangle 51 x 37in on the
burlap. Enlarge and transfer the
design using a marker pen in one color to
draw the grid on the burlap, another to
draw the design, and a third to make
corrections. Allow for a border area of
3in. Mount the burlap on the frame.

2 Choose a selection of appropriate
fabrics such as dense cottons or
woven wools. Cut these into strips,

parallel to the grain of the fabric, about
1in wide x 3½in long.

YOU WILL NEED

≈ *2 yards burlap for*
  ground fabric
≈ *2 yards burlap for*
  lining fabric
≈ *an assortment of clothes*
  and fabrics
≈ *a prodding tool*
≈ *rotary cutter and*
  cutting mat (optional)
≈ *scissors*
≈ *ruler*
≈ *tape measure*
≈ *string*
≈ *1in-long broad-headed*
  nails
≈ *marker pens in three*
  colors
≈ *latex adhesive*
≈ *rug frame*
≈ *G-clamps*
≈ *trestles*

3 Prod the rug, building up a dense, shaggy pile.

4 When the prodding is complete, remove the rug from the frame and lay it face down on a flat surface. Cut away any surplus burlap, leaving a border of 2in for a hem allowance.

▼ FIRE RUG *prodded rug by Ben Hall (measures 37 x 51in).*

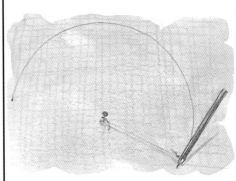

BRIGHT IDEA

To draw a perfect circle, mark a piece of string with half the length of the circle radius. Loop one end of the string around a nail held at the center of the rug. The other end of the string is looped around a marker at the required length and this is then used to draw the circle ≈

5 Place the lining piece of burlap on to the reverse of the rug. Use a marker pen to draw around the rug. Following the marked outline, cut out the lining burlap.

6 Apply a thin layer of latex over the reverse of the rug and leave to dry for five minutes. Press down the hem allowance. At the corners, pinch the excess burlap and miter the edges, using small amounts of latex to stick them into shape. Recoat the hem with latex and allow to dry for three minutes.

7 Lay the burlap backing fabric on to the latexed reverse of the rug, press, and smooth down so that the rug lies flat. Allow to dry overnight. Trim the rug pile so that it is of an even height.

BRAIDED RAG RUGS

▶ FRAGILE STRUCTURES
—THE PLACE *hooked rug
with braided frame
by Nancy Edell
(measures 26 x 30in).*

▶ *Detail of* HEARTH RUG
*project by Juju Vail
(measures 23½ x 36in).*

▶ *Braids make an
attractive border for hooked
rugs. Many old hooked
rugs, such as this Scottie
Dog rug made between
1925 and 1950, include
braided borders
(measures 35 x 29in).*

Braided rugs are made from braided fabric strips stitched together. Braids can be coiled into round or oval shapes, or they can be stitched side-by-side into square mats. A braided rug could be made up of small, braided coils stitched together like quilt blocks.

Fabric strips are usually cut to widths between ½in and 3in wide. A thick braided rug can be made from heavy fabrics, like wool tweeds or coating fabrics, cut into wide strips. For a finer braided rug use a light wool fabric cut into narrow strips.

The fabrics in the braid can change as the rug is made, as they do in our braided rug project. When only one strand of a braid is changed the coloring can be subtle and surprising. Many old rugs are made from similar types of tweed, which change throughout the rug, providing muted colors schemes.

How to Braid

1 Fasten the ends of three strips of fabric together with a safety pin and hook the pin over a cup hook screwed into something secure just above eye level.

2 Start braiding near the pin by bringing the right-hand strip over the middle strip, then the left strip over the new middle strip. Continue braiding, turning raw edges under as much as you can. When you are finished, secure the loose ends with a pin.

Stitching the Braid Together

Using a carpet needle and a heavy linen thread, sew first through the loop of one braid and then through the loop lying beside it.

Work back and forth between the braids, taking care that they remain flat and that the stitching is firm but not too tight. Continue until your rug reaches its final size.

Tapering the Braid

To achieve a smooth finish on the edge of the rug, taper the last 10 inches of each strip to about half the normal width. Finish the braiding and slip the tapered ends into the loop lying beside them. Secure in place, hiding the raw edges.

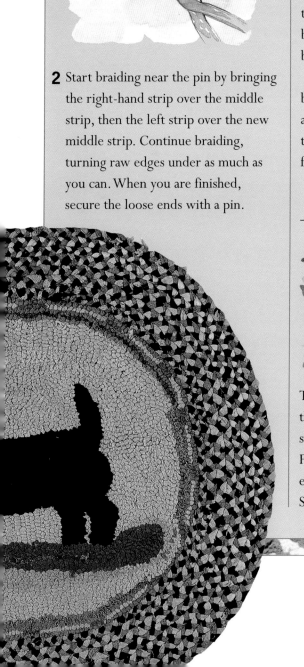

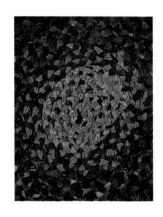

BRAIDED RUG ⊠

JENNI STUART-ANDERSON USED FABRICS WITH A PILE, SUCH AS VELVETS AND CORDUROYS, TO
MAKE THIS BRAIDED RUG. IT HAS A PLUSHER, RICHER LOOK THAN IS COMMONLY ASSOCIATED
WITH THE HOME-SPUN LOOK OF BRAIDED RUGS, MAKING IT SUITABLE FOR A VARIETY OF
LOCATIONS AROUND THE HOME.

YOU WILL NEED

- ≈ *assortment of velvet and*
  corduroy fabrics or
  clothes
- ≈ *1 yard cotton lining*
  fabric
- ≈ *tape measure*
- ≈ *ruler*
- ≈ *scissors*
- ≈ *carpet needle*
- ≈ *heavy linen thread*
- ≈ *safety pin*
- ≈ *pins*
- ≈ *sewing thread to match*
  lining fabric

1 Select fabrics of a similar weight
which look good together. This rug is
made from dress-weight corduroy and
velvet fabrics. Cut the fabric or garment
into 2in wide strips. Try to get pieces of
about a yard long. If your fabric is not that
long, sew strips end to end and trim the
seams to ¼in.

2 Fasten the ends of the three strips
together with a safety pin and hook
the pin over a cup hook screwed into
something secure just above eye level.
Braid until you have about 8in left
unbraided, then secure the loose ends
with a pin.

3 Remove the safety pin and stitch the
ends neatly together, concealing the
raw edges within the braid.

NOTE
Stagger the seams in the strips to avoid lumps in the braids ≈

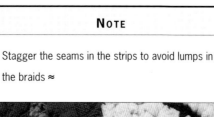

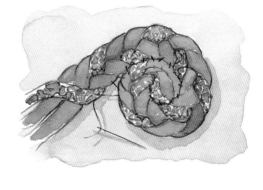

4 Take the joined end of the braid and
start coiling it into a flat circle.
Working with the spiral flat on the table,
stitch the beginning of the braid to an
adjacent bit of braid. Do not pull the thread
too tight or your rug will not be flat.

5 Continue to stitch through an edge of
one braid, then through an edge of
the adjacent braid, so that the stitches do
not show. Every 2½in, pass the needle
right through the braid and back again to
secure it to the spiral. Avoid pulling the
thread so tightly that it deforms the braid.

6 Near the end of the braid, sew on
more strips. Braid them, sew more of
the spiral, adding strips as you go. In this
way you can select and change colors in
relation to the growing rug.

7 When the rug reaches the desired size (this one measures 31½in diameter), taper the fabric strips to about half their normal width over about 10in. Braid the tapered ends and stitch them to the rug so that the braid tapers neatly against the edge.

8 Place the rug on your lining fabric and cut around it leaving 1in hem allowance all around.

9 Turn the rug upside-down and pin the lining on to it, turning under the hem allowance as you stitch.

10 Use a rug back stitch to hold the lining in place. Stitch parallel lines, running every 2in across the back of the rug. This will help to hold the braids firmly together.

11 Turn under a hem on the outside edge of the lining and attach it to the rug using ladder stitch.

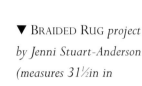

▼ BRAIDED RUG *project by Jenni Stuart-Anderson (measures 31½in in diameter).*

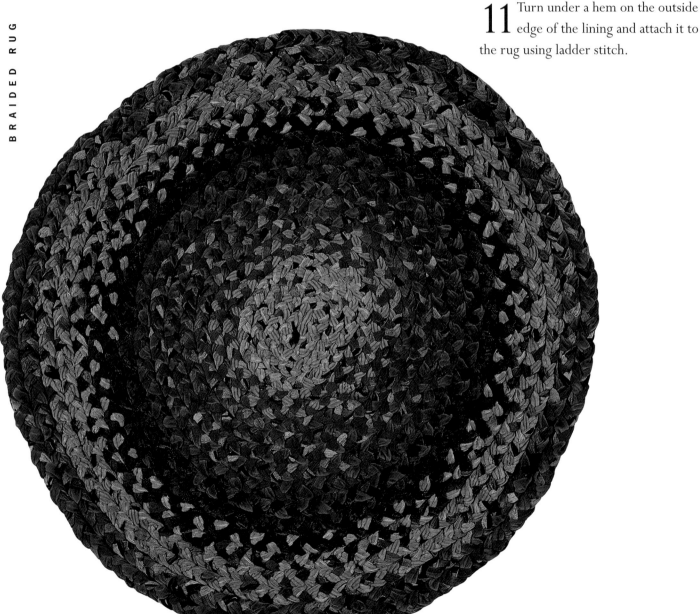

HEARTH RUG

THIS RUG LOOKS WELCOMING PLACED AT THE DOOR TO A ROOM OR IN FRONT OF A FIRE. ALTHOUGH THE SILK ROSETTES ADD A DECORATIVE FINISHING TOUCH THEY ARE PROBABLY BEST NOT USED IN A RUG THAT GETS HEAVY, DIRTY TRAFFIC. THE EDGES OF THE ROSES ARE NOT HEMMED AS THEIR FRAYED EDGES ARE SYMPATHETIC WITH THE HOOKING. THE BRAID COULD HAVE BEEN CREATED FROM MANY DIFFERENT FABRICS TO GIVE THE RUG A MORE VIBRANT FINISH.

1 The hooked part of the rug measures 31 x 19in. Enlarge and transfer the design using a marker pen in one color to draw the grid on the burlap, another to draw the design, and a third color to make corrections. Allow for a border area of at least 3in. Mount the burlap on the hooking frame.

2 To make the roses, select two pieces of fabric, one for the center of each rose and one for the outside. Cut a strip for the center of the rose 3 x 3in and one for the outside of the rose 3 x 10in. Stitch the strips together to make one continuous strip 3in wide by 11½in long, with a seam allowance of ¾in.

BRIGHT IDEA

To add dots of color around the flowers carry long strips of fabric or a furry yarn across the back of the rug, pulling it through the pile where needed ≈

YOU WILL NEED

≈ 1 yard burlap for ground fabric

≈ 1 yard cotton lining fabric

≈ an assortment of silk rags (or similar fabric)

≈ assortment of clothes and fabrics, including a variety of wool tweeds

≈ 3 garments in denim and tweed fabrics

≈ scissors

≈ carpet needle

≈ heavy-linen thread

≈ safety pin

≈ pins

≈ sewing thread

≈ a primitive size hook

≈ marker pens in three colors

≈ latex adhesive

≈ rug frame

≈ G-clamps (optional)

≈ trestles (optional)

3 Starting at the center of the rose, with the seam on the underside, wrap the strip into a rosette. Gather, fold, and pin the silk as you work and tuck the end of the strip underneath the rosette. Tack the folds in place using a neutral color sewing thread. Make sure the rosette is firmly secured before you remove the pins. Repeat these instructions for each of the roses.

4 Hook the four 'daisies' by pulling the loops extra long to make the petals. Hook the leaves, basket, and background. Add dots of other colors to give the impression of smaller flowers.

5 To make the striped band around the outside of the hooking, hook strips of a variety of rags so that they radiate from the center of the rug.

6 When the hooking is complete make the braids from the tweed and denim fabrics. Cut the fabric into 2in-wide strips. Sew the strips end to end making three strips of about one yard long. Trim the seams to ¼in. Fasten the ends of the three strips together with a safety pin and hook the pin over a cup hook screwed into something secure just above eye level.

7 Start braiding near the pin by bringing the right-hand strip over the middle strip, then the left strip over the new middle strip. Continue braiding, turning raw edges under as much as you can, until you have about 8in left unbraided. Secure the loose ends with a pin.

8 Stitch the braid to the rug while it is still mounted on the rug frame. This will help the rug to lie flat and not warp. Leave the first 2in of the braid free and begin stitching the rest of the braid, edge to edge with the rug. Be careful not to stitch through the unhooked burlap, as this will be folded under the hooking when the rug is complete. You will need to sew right through the braid occasionally to hold it.

9 Near the end of the braid, sew on more strips staggering the joins. Braid them, then continue sewing the braid to the rug.

10 As you come to the end of the first row of braiding overlap the first 2in of braid that was left free. Continue the braid until you have two complete rows. To finish the braid, continue it for 3in more and tuck it under the braiding. Tack the braid in place.

NOTE

Do not pull the thread so tightly that it deforms the braid ≈

NOTE

The braiding fabrics could be changed for the second row of braiding ≈

11 Remove the rug from the frame and lay it face down on a flat surface. Cut away any surplus burlap, leaving a hem allowance of 2in. Clip so that it will curve when folded under the rug.

12 Place the rug on the cotton lining fabric and cut around it leaving 2in for the hem allowance.

13 Apply a thin layer of latex to the hooking on the reverse of the rug and leave to dry for five minutes. Then press the burlap hem down. Allow to dry.

14 Turn the rug upside-down and pin the cotton lining in place, turning under the hem allowance.

15 Use a rug back stitch to hold the lining in place. Stitch in lines across the braids to hold them firmly together.

16 Turn hem under on the outside edge of the lining and attach this to the rug using ladder stitch.

▼ HEARTH RUG
*project by Juju Vail
(measures 23½ x 36in).*

APPLIQUÉ
RAG RUGS

The tradition of making appliquéd rugs pre-dates hooked and prodded rugs. They were often used as table and bed covers in nineteenth century North America. Patchwork rugs, made from blocks of appliqué, were common; some depicted folk art motifs such as hearts, stars, flowers, and animals while others were simple geometric blocks.

◀ Detail from MOSAIC FELT RUG *by Rachel MacHenry.*

▲ Herringbone stitch is used to hold the blocks of plaid suiting fabrics together in this old appliquéd rug (measures 42 x 25in).

Old appliquéd rugs were made by sewing felt segments to a ground fabric. A feature was made of the stitches by using contrasting colored yarns. Today the process of appliqué can be made faster with the use of a double-sided fusing, such as Wonder-under or Bondaweb. Although

HOW TO FELT WOOL FABRICS

Wool sweaters are ideal for felting but any pure wool fabric is suitable. You need some old towels, laundry soap, and a washer and drier.

1 To prepare wool clothes for felting cut off the ribbings, buttons, pockets, edgings, seams, and trims. Cut the sleeves off the bodies and cut the bodies open at side and shoulder seams.

2 Load the wool pieces, the old towels, (which should make up a third of the washing load) and the washing soap into a washing machine. Wash on a 'hot' or 'hot/cold' washing cycle.

3 Put everything, including the towels, into a dryer and spin on a hot setting for about 20 minutes. If the fabric is not sufficiently felted, repeat the washing and drying process.

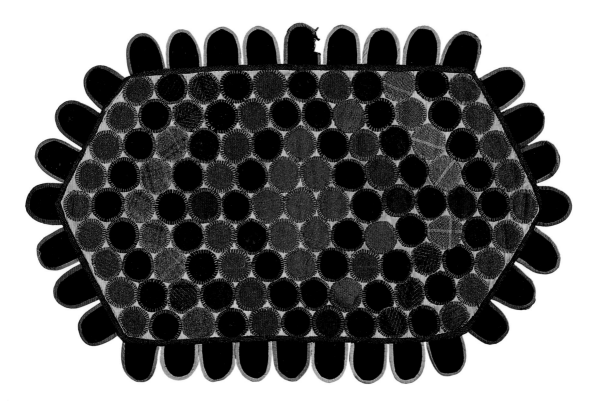

a decorative stitch is still desirable, double-sided fusing allows the rug maker to hold a design composition in place while it is stitched.

Double-sided fusing is a webbing fabric with glue impregnated on both sides of the fabric. It works like double-sided tape, sticking one fabric to another. Most double-sided fusings come on sheets of thin paper. You place the felt wrong side up, then position the glued side of the paper on top of it. To transfer the glue on to the fabric, iron over the paper, following the manufacturer's instructions for the correct iron setting and timing. Next, peel off the paper. Turn the fabric pieces over so that they are right side up and glue side down, and position them on the background fabric. Once you are satisfied with their position, iron each piece on to the background, pressing over a damp cloth. You may need to turn the

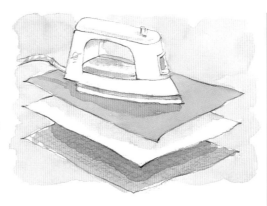

piece upside-down and iron over the backing material if your felt is very thick.

Traditional rugs from around the world are made from felt. It is a hard-wearing fabric that stands up to use on the floor. Felt is made from pure wool fibers exposed to heat, moisture, and agitation which fuse the wool fibers into a fabric. You can use store-bought felt to make appliquéd rugs or you can felt your own fabrics from knitted and woven pure wools.

▲ *Woolen penny rugs were constructed of cloth 'pennies' made from men's suiting fabrics and coarse blanketing. The 'pennies' were blanket stitched to a woolen ground fabric and sometimes further embellished with embroidery (measures 30 x 45in).*

EMBROIDERY STITCHES

Traditional felt appliquéd rugs used blanket and herringbone stitch in wool yarns to decorate the surface and hold the appliquéd pieces in place. However, any embroidery stitch could be used.

Blanket Stitch

Blanket stitch was used around the outside edge of felt circles to decorate them and hold them in place on a ground fabric. To embellish a felt rug with blanket stitch, use a contrasting color thread for strong visual impact. Working with the right side

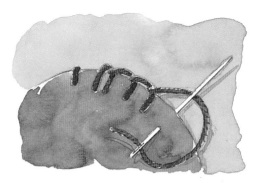

of the fabric facing you, fasten the working thread just under the fabric edge and insert the needle the desired distance at right angles to the edge. Take a stitch through the fabric, looping the working thread behind the needle before pulling it through to form a loop on the edge of the appliquéd fabric.

▼ *This shaggy scalloped rug was made by stitching one edge of a knitted strip to the rug in a spiral fashion. The knit was then unraveled to produce a curly yarn pile. The appliquéd scallops on this rug are made from men's suiting and bound with dress fabrics (measures 23 x 36in).*

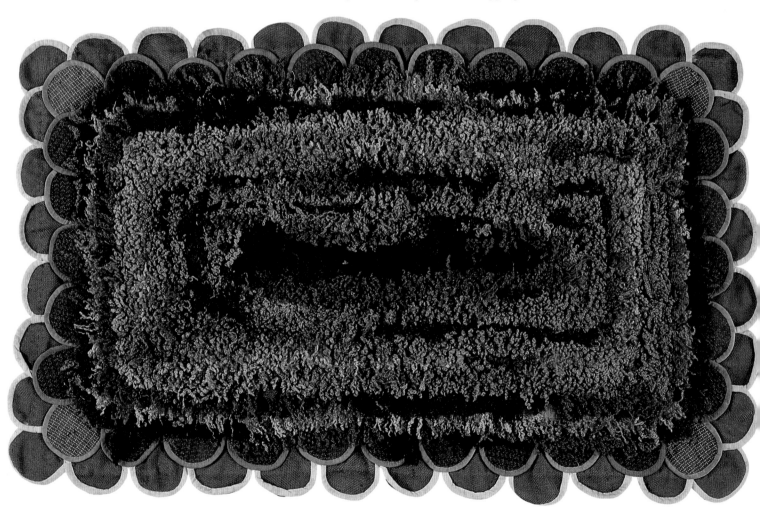

Herringbone Stitch

Herringbone stitch was used to hold two pieces of felt together. Fabric blocks were pinned edge to edge on a ground fabric and a herringbone stitch was embroidered over the edges, through all layers of fabric, holding the seam in place.

Machine Embroidery

Felt pieces can also be secured to a ground fabric using machine embroidery instead of herringbone stitch.

Use a thread that matches the color of your felt. Place two pieces of felt, edge to edge, on a burlap ground fabric then stitch using the machine's widest zigzag setting.

▼ *An old cornmeal sack was used as a ground fabric for this felt appliqué rug. A Velcro strip, stitched to the lining fabric on the wrong side, is used to affix the rug to the wall for displaying.*

▲ *This appliquéd rug is made in blocks that have been pieced together with herringbone stitch. Each block has flower shapes made of small circles of felt held to a woolen ground fabric with cross stitch (measures 43 x 24in, mid-twentieth century).*

PIECED FELT RUG 🦎

RACHEL MACHENRY WAS INSPIRED BY OLD FELT EMBROIDERIES, APPLIQUÉD RUGS, AND WORKMEN'S QUILTS WHEN MAKING THIS RUG. A WASHING MACHINE, DRIER, AND DOUBLE-SIDED FUSING MAKE TRADITIONAL FELT APPLIQUÉ TECHNIQUES MORE PRACTICAL. THE DIMENSIONS AND COLORS OF THIS RUG CAN EASILY BE ALTERED TO YOUR OWN FABRICS AND INTERIOR DECOR.

YOU WILL NEED

≈ *a selection of pure wool knitted or woven clothes in solid colors*

≈ *old towels*

≈ *soft laundry soap*

≈ *washing machine and drier*

≈ *double-sided fusing*

≈ *20 white pearl buttons*

≈ *embroidery threads in assortment of colors*

≈ *1½ yards burlap lining fabric*

≈ *sewing machine*

≈ *black and neutral sewing threads*

≈ *needle*

≈ *scissors*

≈ *iron*

≈ *rotary cutter and mat*

≈ *ruler*

≈ *black marker*

1 Felt an assortment of pure wool knitted and woven garments.

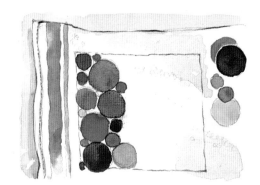

2 To make section A, mark a guideline on an old towel, 18½ x 9in. Using a selection of tin cans, cups, mugs, and thread spools as templates cut a range of circle sizes from the felted fabrics.

3 The design will be arranged with the wrong side facing. Arrange the largest circles, according to the design, within the guidelines marked on the towel.

4 Cut a piece of double-sided fusing 18½ x 9in and place it on top of the felt circles. Cut a piece of burlap 20½ x 11in and place it on top of the fusing. Press according to the manufacturer's directions.

5 Turn the rug over so that you can see the right side. Fill in the holes with smaller circles of felt. They will distort to fill the spaces when fused. Press the rug on the right side, then turn it over and press on the wrong side. Machine stitch around the outside edges of the circles through all the layers, using a zigzag stitch in a neutral colored thread. Press the rug lightly, with a steam iron.

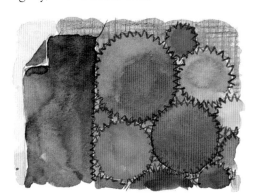

6 To make section B cut two pieces 11¾ x 2¾in and two pieces 24½ x 2¾in from black felt. Join the shorter pieces to the sides of section A by placing the fabrics right side up next to each other and zigzag stitching the edges together. Then join the longer pieces to the top and bottom of section A in the same way and press lightly.

7 Prepare sections C and D by cutting 16 strips of felt 2 x 12in. Sew them into segments, each with eight strips, by placing the fabrics right side up, next to each other and zigzag stitching the edges together. Prepare sections E and F by cutting 54 strips of felt 2 x 5½in. Sew them into segments, each with 27 strips, and press lightly.

8 Join segments C and D to the sides of the rug with a zigzag stitch. Then join segments E and F across the top and bottom of the rug with zigzag stitch.

9 Cut a border for the rug 1in in width, piecing if necessary so that it fits around the outside of the rug. Zigzag stitch the border around the edge of rug and press lightly.

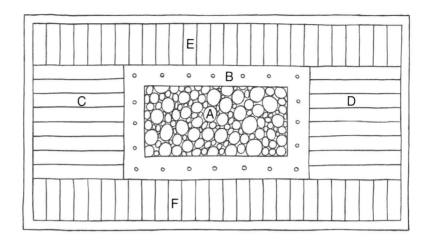

10 Place the rug on top of the lining fabric. Cut out the lining, leaving a 1in seam allowance. Stitch the lining in place, turning under a hem and press lightly.

11 Stitch pearl buttons on to the border section B with embroidery threads, sewing through all layers.

▶ *Felt appliquéd cushions and rugs by Rachel MacHenry.*

▼ PIECED FELT RUG *project by Rachel MacHenry (measures 48 x 26in).*

MOSAIC FELT RUG

THIS PIECED FELT RUG BY RACHEL MacHENRY WAS INSPIRED BY MOSAICS. HEART OR STAR SHAPES COULD BE ADDED TO OR SUBSTITUTED FOR THE MOON SHAPES IN THE MOSAIC. THE DEEP JEWEL COLORS CAN BE FOUND IN AN ASSORTMENT OF SECOND-HAND KNITTED SWEATERS, DRESSES, AND VESTS.

1 Prepare the rug by felting an assortment of wool garments. Cut a 43 x 29in piece of burlap for the lining.

2 To make the central 'mosaic' motif of the rug you will need to make four square units, two of a cool range of colors (blues, cool violets, greens, and purples) and two of a warm range (soft pinks, yellows, reds, and oranges). Select cool toned colors and cut them into five ¾in strips. Cut these strips into little squares and triangles and repeat the process with five warm colors.

3 Make one 11in square of the central motif at a time. On an old towel, mark an 11in square with the black marker to serve as a guideline. Cut a 12in square of burlap and another of the double-sided fusing and set aside.

> **NOTE**
>
> When cutting 'mosaic' squares and triangles, don't be too precise. These look better when they show some variety ≈

> **NOTE**
>
> The 'mosaic' design will be worked first, then a layer of the double-sided fusing. The burlap will then be applied on top of both previous layers and fused from the back with an iron. The felt is too thick to iron it from the front ≈

4 Cut moon-shaped pieces from black felt. Place them on the towel within the marked guidelines.

> **NOTE**
>
> All the measurements given correspond to the rug shown here. As you make the rug, the felt may change shape, so it is best to cut the pieces as you go to accommodate any change in the rug dimensions as you work ≈

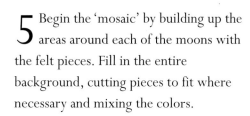

5 Begin the 'mosaic' by building up the areas around each of the moons with the felt pieces. Fill in the entire background, cutting pieces to fit where necessary and mixing the colors.

YOU WILL NEED

- ≈ *2 yards burlap*
- ≈ *a selection of pure wool knitted or woven clothes in solid colors*
- ≈ *old towels*
- ≈ *soft laundry soap*
- ≈ *washing machine and drier*
- ≈ *double-sided fusing*
- ≈ *20 white pearl buttons*
- ≈ *embroidery threads in assortment of colors*
- ≈ *sewing machine*
- ≈ *black thread*
- ≈ *neutral colored thread (such as light brown)*
- ≈ *needle*
- ≈ *scissors*
- ≈ *iron*
- ≈ *rotary cutter and mat*
- ≈ *black marker pen*

6 Place the double-sided fusing and the burlap over the mosaic and steam press according to the manufacturer's instructions.

7 Using a neutral colored thread, machine quilt all the layers together. Follow the shapes of the moons, creating a swirling pattern with the stitching.

8 Make three more squares, so that there are two made from cool colors and two made from warm colors. Trim the burlap close to the mosaic.

9 Pin the four square 'mosaic' sections to the center of the burlap lining fabric. Place them as close together as possible, with the two cool colored squares diagonal to one another. Fill in any gaps and cover the burlap edges with felt squares using scraps of the double-sided fusing.

10 Zigzag stitch, with a neutral colored thread the four 'mosaic' squares edge to edge with each other, through the burlap lining fabric. Zigzag stitch the outside edge of the four squares to the rug lining.

▶ MOSAIC FELT RUG
project by Rachel MacHenry (measures 46 x 31 in).

11 Cut strips of black felt 1in wide, to border the 'mosaic' section. Pin the border to the burlap lining and zigzag stitch the edge of the border to the edge of the mosaic using a black thread.

12 Prepare two sections of 21 stripes each (or enough to fit the edges of your rug.) Cut 42 strips 1¼ x 8½in in various colors of felt. Arrange these in stripes to fit the sides of the rug. Join the strips by zigzag stitching them edge to edge, then steam press gently. Zigzag stitch each band of 21 stripes edge to edge with the border, stitching through the burlap lining.

13 Make the edge strip for the top and bottom of the mosaic area out of rectangles of random widths. Stitch these to the upper and lower borders. Zigzag stitch the outside edge of the rug to the burlap lining. Trim away any excess burlap. Zigzag stitch another border of 1in to the outside edge of the rug using the black thread.

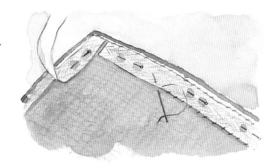

14 Ladder stitch a 1in-wide twill tape over the edge of the burlap on the back of rug. Steam press the rug gently.

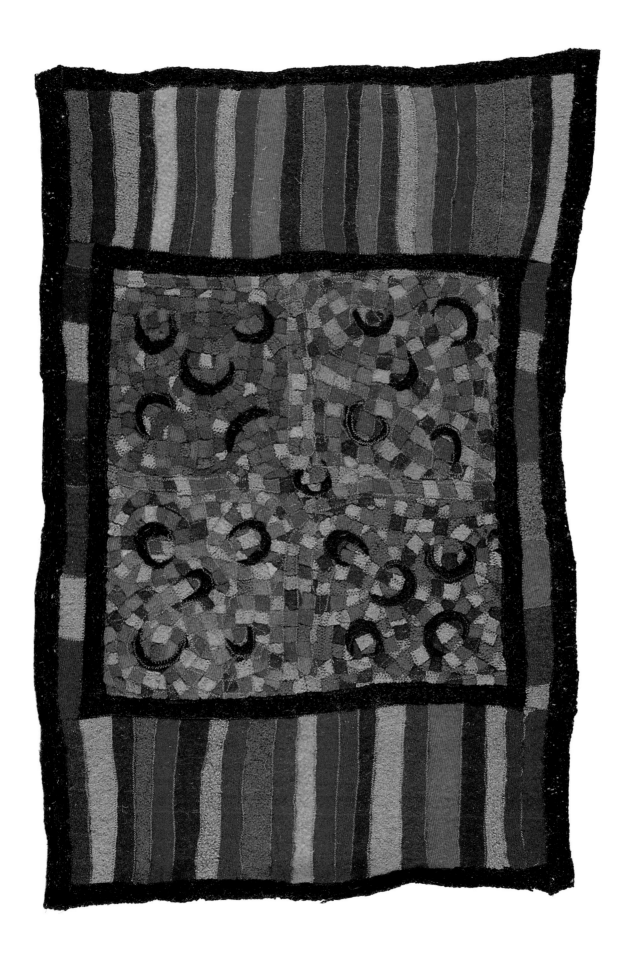

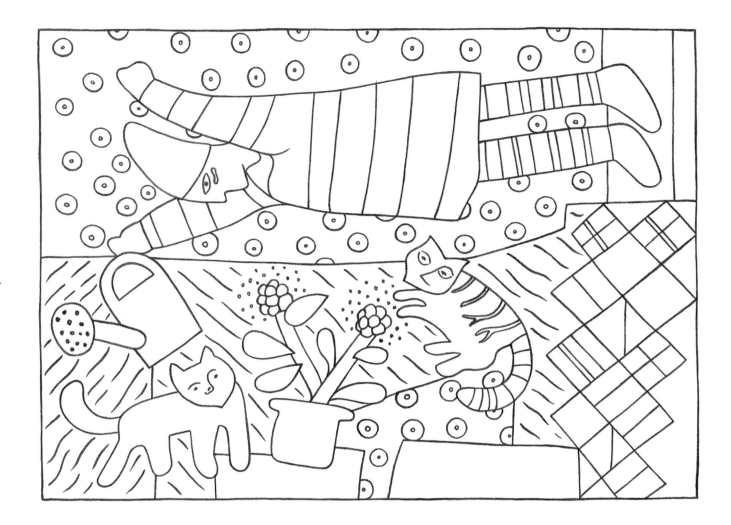

Place an acetate grid marked with 1-inch squares over the rug diagram. Multiply each square by the scale factor to enlarge the rug design to full size.

▲ The Flying Gardener Rug, page 36
Actual size 44 x 30in
Enlarge 6 times

◀ Hen in the Garden Rug, page 39
Actual size 30 x 42in
Enlarge 8.4 times

▶ Heart Rug, page 44
Actual size 37½ x 27in
Enlarge 4 times

▶ Cottage Garden Rug,
page 58
Actual size 42 x 39in
Enlarge 8 times

◀ There was Nothing on it but Tea Picture,
page 50
Actual size 24 x 24in
Enlarge 5.6 times

▶ Hooked Hat, page 54
Actual size 3¼ x 25¾in
Enlarge 2.6 times

TEMPLATES

◀ Golden Hamstrings
Runner, page 47
Actual size 65 x 28in
Enlarge 7.5 times

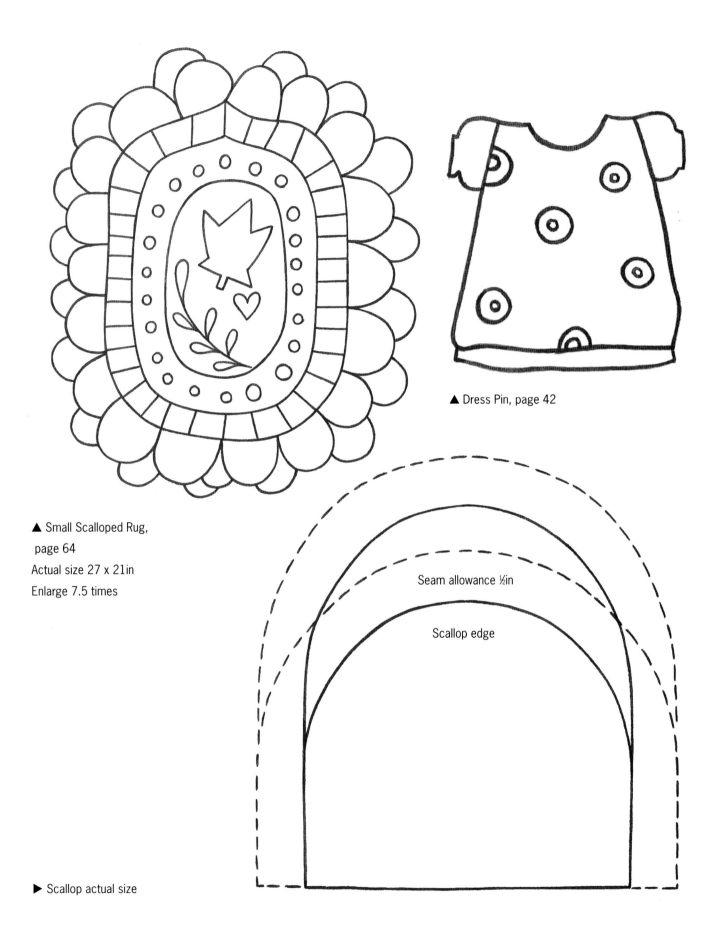

TEMPLATES

▲ Dress Pin, page 42

▲ Small Scalloped Rug,
  page 64
Actual size 27 x 21in
Enlarge 7.5 times

Seam allowance ½in

Scallop edge

▶ Scallop actual size

◀ Whale Rug,
page 61
Actual size 60 x 35
Enlarge 10 times

▼ Angel Bench Cushion,
page 71
Actual size 21 x 15½in
Enlarge 3.4 times

▶ Diamond Rug,
page 77
Actual size 60 x 36in
Enlarge 11 times

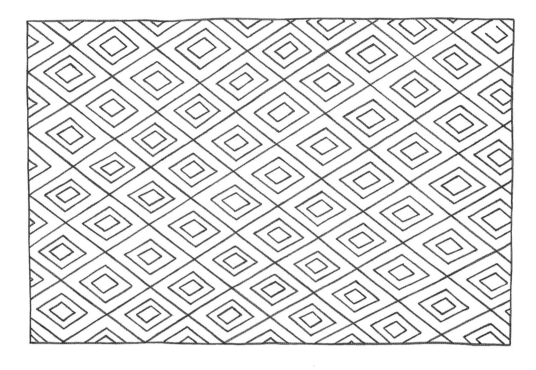

▼ Neo-classical Rug,
page 74
Actual size 30 x 50in
Enlarge 7 times

▲ Moonlit Forest Rug,
page 86
Actual size 74 x 45½in
Enlarge 10.5 times

◀ Fire Rug
Actual size 37 x 51in
Enlarge 9.5 times

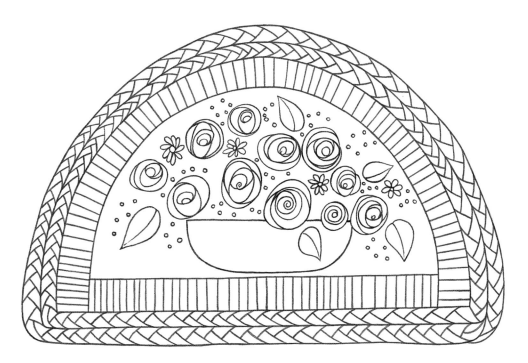

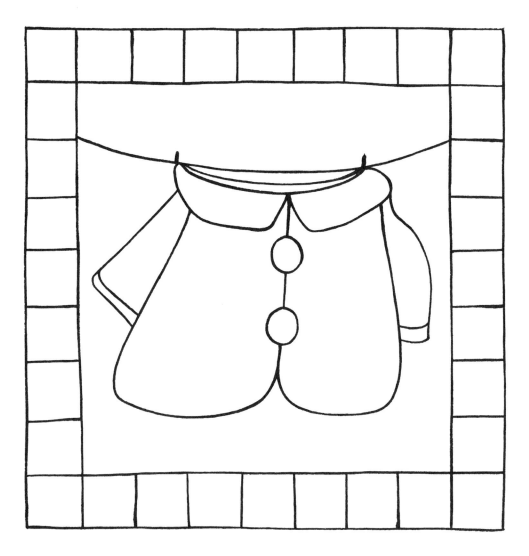

TEMPLATES

◄ Hearth Rug,
page 99
Actual size 23½ x 36in
Enlarge 6.7 times

► Mosaic Felt Rug,
 page 112
Actual size 46 x 31in
Enlarge 6.9 times

◄ Coat on a Line Picture,
page 68
Actual size 27 x 27in
Enlarge 5 times

► Pieced Felt Rug,
page 108
Actual size 48 x 26in
Enlarge 7.25 times

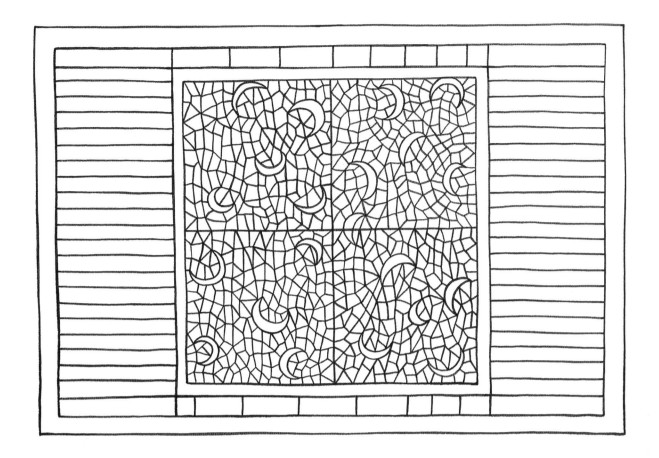

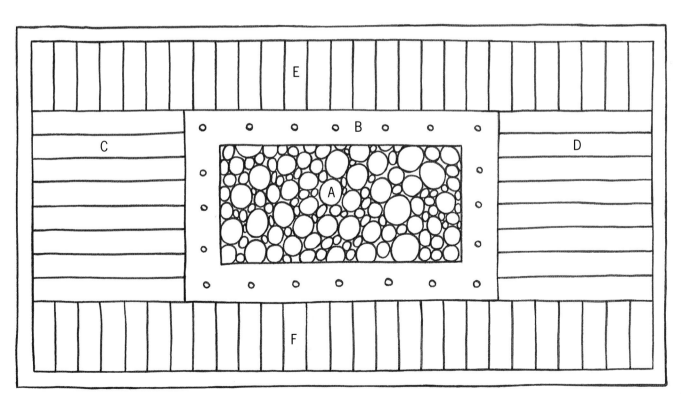

APPENDIX

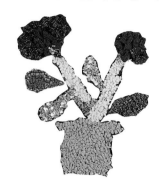

▲ ROSIE ON BEN NICHOLSON CUSHION
hooked rug by Louisa Creed
(measures 36 x 51in).

Artists' Addresses

Louisa Creed
27 York Norfolk Street
York YO2 1JY U.K.

Nancy Edell
R.R.#1 Bayswater
Hubbards, Nova Scotia
B0J 1T0 Canada

Ben Hall
56 Glenwood Road, Flat 2
London SE6 4NF U.K.

Liz Kitching
Hill Cottage, Walton
Brampton
Cumbria CA8 2EA U.K.

Barbara Klunder
12 First Street
Toronto Island
M5J 2A6 Canada

Anita Langham
'Ebor Ruggers
c/o Yorkshire Museum of Farming
Murton, York U.K.

Susan Lindsay
44½ Victoria Park Avenue
Toronto, Ontario
M4E 3R9 Canada

Rachel MacHenry
148 Clinton Street
Toronto, Ontario
M6G 2Y3 Canada

Lu Mason
86 Lindley Street
York YO2 4JF U.K.

Janice McLaren
96D Bethune Road
London N16 5BA U.K.

Chris Oakenfull
13 East Mount Road
York
North Yorks YO2 2BD U.K.

Lizzie Reakes
68 Oaklands Road
London W7 2DU U.K.

▼ *Selection of rag rugs on Chinese cabinet.*

▲ LIFE RUG *hooked rug by Anita Langham. This rug, made to celebrate a birthday, was hooked in bands so that the maker never ran out of fabrics (measures 79 x 39in).*

Jenni Stuart-Anderson
The Birches
Middleton-on-the-Hill
Herefordshire HR6 0H2 U.K.

Lynne Stein
4 Oakdale Court
Grey Road, Altrincham
Cheshire WA14 4BX U.K.

Amanda Townend
150 Barlow Moor Road
West Didsbury
Manchester M20 2UT U.K.

Jan Tricker
Dolphin House, 18 Hale Street
Staines
Middlesex TW18 4UW U.K.

Juju Vail
6 Alconbury Road
London E5 8RH U.K.

Suppliers

CANADA

The Wool Winder
RR#1,
Manilla, Ontario
K0M 2J0
Tel: (705) 786-1358
Complete line of rug-hooking and braiding supplies.

GREAT BRITAIN AND IRELAND

Farmhouse Frames
Christine Birch
Pen yr Allt Farm
Llanrhychwyn
Above Trefriw
Gwynedd, LL27 0YX
Wales
Tel: (01492) 640881
Suppliers of custom-made frames and rug-making tools.

Lynne Stein
4 Oakdale Court
Grey Road
Altrincham
Cheshire WA14 4BX
England
Tel: (0161) 941 5315
Mail order supplier of rug frames, and tools.

Neville Smith
Ballincur, Clogh
Gorey, Co. Wexford
Ireland
Tel: (353) 55 20927
Makers of rug tools of brass and yew. Trade orders and individual designs welcome.

Russell & Chapple Ltd.
23 Monmouth Street
Shaftesbury Avenue
London WC2H 9DE
England
Tel: (0171) 836 7521 Fax: (0171) 497 0554
Retail and mail order suppliers of burlap fabrics.

Studio Rugworks
Duvals Farm House
White Lane
Hawkhurst, Kent TN18 5DD
England
Tel: (01580) 753315
Mail order supplier of tools and materials, including punch needle and monks cloth.

Whaleys (Bradford) Ltd.
Harris Court
Great Horton
Bradford
West Yorkshire
BD7 4EQ
England
Tel: (01274) 576718
Fax: (01274) 521309
Mail order suppliers of fabrics.

▲ JENNY'S RUG *based on her daughter's drawings by Chris Oakenfull (measures 32 x 39*

U.S.A.

Braid-Aid
466 Washington Street
P.O. Box 603
Pembroke, MA 02359
Tel: (617) 826-2560
Extensive rug-making supplies.

Gloria E. Crouse
4325 John Luhr Road N.E.
Olympia, Washington 98516-2320
Tel: (360) 491 1980
Mail order supplier of rug-making tools and materials.

The Ruggery
565 Cedar Swamp Road
Glen Head, NY 11535
Tel: (516) 676-2056
Supply extensive range of rug-making materials including punch needles.

▲ OWEN FRANCIS *hooked rug by Lu Mason, (measures 72 x 36in).*

Guilds and Associations

American Craft Council
40 West 53rd Street
New York NY 10019 U.S.A.
Tel: (212) 274 0630

Association of Rag Rug Makers
1 Wingrad House
Jubilee Street
London E1 3BJ U.K.

British Crafts Council
44a Pentonville Road
London N1 9BY U.K.
Tel: (0171) 278 7700

The International Guild of Handhooking
Rugmakers
Carol Harvey-Clark
R.R.#3
Bridgewater, Nova Scotia
B4V 2W2 Canada
Write to Carol Harvey-Clark for information and a contact name in your country or area.

Magazine

Rug Hooking
Commonwealth
Communication Services, Inc.
P.O. Box 15760
Harrisburg, PA 17105 U.S.A.

Internet

http//gpu.srv.ualberta.ca/~dmerriam/hooked.html

Places to Visit

CANADA

Art Gallery of Nova Scotia
1741 Hollis Street
P.O. Box 2262
Halifax, Nova Scotia
B3J 3C8

Canadian Craft Museum
639 Hornby Street
Vancouver, British Columbia
V6C 2G3
Tel: (604) 687 8266

McCord Museum of Canadian History
690 Sherbrooke Street West
Montreal, Quebéc
H3A 1E9

Museum for Textiles
55 Centre Avenue
Toronto, Ontario
M5G 2H5
Tel: (416) 599 5321

New Brunswick Museum
277 Douglas Avenue
Saint John, Newfoundland
A1C 5S7

Royal Ontario Museum
100 Queen's Park
Toronto, Ontario
M5S 2C6
Tel: (416) 586 5549

GREAT BRITAIN

American Museum
Claverton Manor
Bath
Avon BA2 7BD

Beamish Open Air Museum
Beamish
Nr. Chester-le-Street
Co. Durham DH9 0RG

East Riddlesden Hall
Bradford Road
Keighley
Yorkshire BD20 5EL

Highland Folk Museum
Duke Street
Kingussie
Inverness

Ryedale Folk Museum
Hutton-le-Hole
York

Shipley Art Gallery
Prince Consort Road
Gateshead
Tyne & Wear

▲ TANAKA STORY *hooked rug by Barbara Klunder, (measures 72 x 48in).*

U.S.A.

Bybee Collection
Dallas Art Museum
1717 North Harwood
Dallas TX 75201
Tel: (214) 922 1200

Hancock Shaker Village
Route 20
Pittsfield Albany Road
Pittsfield, MA 01202

Henry Ford Museum
20900 Oakwood Boulevard
PO Box 1970
Dearborn, MI 48121-1970
Tel: (313) 271 1620

Museum of American Folk Art
49 West 53rd Street
New York, NY 10019

Shaker Museum
95 Shaker Museum Road
Old Chatham, NY 12136

Shelburne Museum
Route 7
PO Box 10
Shelburne, VT 05482
Tel: (802) 985 3344

Society for the Preservation of New
England Antiquities
Beauport House
75 Eastern Point Boulevard
Gloucester, MA 01930
Tel: (508) 283 0800

Wenham Historical Association Museum
132 Main Street
Wenham, MA 01984

ACKNOWLEDGMENTS

The Author and the Publishers would like to thank all the rug makers, past and present, who contributed work to this book.

The following were generous in their help in the production of this book: Sarah Holland, Marion John and Rachel and Thelma MacHenry of the Museum for Textiles in Toronto, Jamie Maxwell and Heidi Bojanc of the Toronto Historical Board, Anna Zaremba, Technographic Equipment Limited of Markham, Ontario (for lighting by Bowens), Trevor Shier of Watermark Resorts, Cambridgeshire.

▶ PEG AND LINE *by Susan Lindsay (measures 23 x 16in).*

INDEX

adhesives 22
appliqued rugs 14, 103–12
    method 104–7
    projects
        Mosaic Felt Rug 111–13,
           123
        Pierced Felt Rug 108–9, 123

braided rugs 14, 93–102
    method 95
    projects
        Braided Rug 96–8
        Hearth Rug *94,* 99–101, 122
burlap backing 13, 22

Canadian traditional hooked rugs
    9, 13, 30, 31, 33
canvas stretchers, use of 20–1, 25
Caswell, Zeruah Higley
    Guernsey 14
Creed, Louisa, rugs by *21, 125*
cutters 20

double-sided fusing, use of
    104–5

Edell, Nancy, rugs by *21, 94*
embroidery 106–7

fabric, choice & preparation 20,
    24, 30–5

felting 104
frames 20–2, 25

ground/backing fabrics 22, 25

Hall, Ben, rugs by *82, 83, 85,*
    89–90
hooked rugs
    evolution & history 9–13, 30
    fabric preparation 20, 24,
        30–5
    hooks 19
    technique 32
    projects
        Angel Bench Cushion
           71–3, 119
        Coat on a Line Picture
           68–70, 122
        Cottage Garden Rug
           58–60, 115
        Dress Pin 42–3, 118
        Diamond Rug 77–9, 120
        Flying Gardener Children's
           Rug 36–8, 114
        Golden Hamstrings
           Runner 47–9, 117
        Heart Rug 44–6, 115
        Hen in the Garden Rug
           39–41, 114
        Hooked Hat 54–7, 116
        Neo-Classical Rug 74–6, 120

Small Scalloped Rug
    64–7, 118
"There was Nothing on it but
    Tea" Picture 50–3, 115

Kitching, Liz, rug by 58–9
Klunder, Barbara, rugs by *7, 10,*
    15, 127

Langham, Anita, rugs by *10, 125*
Lindsay, Susan, rugs by *8, 35,*
    42–3, 68–70, 125, 127
linen backing 13, 22
lining 22, 26–7

MacHenry, Rachel, rugs by *103,*
    108–9, 110, 111–13
McLaren, Janice, rugs by *7, 18*
Mason, Lu, rugs by *16,* 77–9, *126*
materials 22–4, 30–5

needles 22

Oakenfull, Chris, rug by *6,* 125

pile 35
prodded rugs 14, 81–90
    technique 84
    tools 19
    projects
        Fire Rug 89–90, 121

Moonlit Forest Rug 86–8,
    121

Reakes, Lizzie, rugs by *22, 33, 47–9*

Stein, Lynne, rugs by *1 11, 15,*
    50–3, 74–6
stitches, embroidery
    Blanket Stitch 106
    Herringbone Stitch 107
    Machine Embroidery 107
stitches, structural
    Herringbone Stitch 27
    Ladder Stitch 27
    Rug Back Stitch 26–7
    Slip Stitch 27
strippers 20
Stuart-Anderson, Jenni, rugs by
    10, 96–8

tools 19–22
Tremblay, George Edouard 12
Townend, Amanda, rugs by
    44–6, *84, 128*
Tricker, Jan, rug by 61–3

Vail, Juju (author), rugs by *17,* 36–8,
    54–7, 64–9, 74–6, *94,* 99–101

Warning, Maria, rugs by *9, 25, 30*
working position 26

▲ HEARTS AND FLOWERS *hooked rug by Amanda Townend (measures 30 x 9in).*

128